THE NEXT 70 DAYS

A DTS Re-Entry Devotional

TANYA LYONS

Tanya Lyons Publishing

Printed in the United States of America

First Printing, 2018

ISBN 978-1-7752712-0-8

Cover design by Leah Sands

Printed by CreateSpace, An Amazon.com Company

Contents

Introduction

If you are reading this book, you have most likely attended one of Youth With A Mission's (YWAM) Discipleship Training Schools (DTS) somewhere in the world. Those five to six months of DTS have become an important part of your life and history, and this devotional book is written for you.

Returning to "normal life" after DTS is not easy at all. I'm glad it's not easy. I hope it's not easy. My hope is that what you experienced in DTS will have long-lasting results in your life. I hope what you experienced in DTS will change the way you relate to others, connect with God, view yourself, spend your money, use your time, make decisions, serve people around you, and so much more. I hope your experience in DTS will push you to think more deeply about the simple decisions you make every day, and that you will continue to invite God to be part of them.

Some of you who are reading this were doing many things well before you went to DTS. I applaud you! I'm glad there were people in your life to teach you the ways of faith. The community you've been a part of, the examples you've had, the safe places where you've been able to grow—these are all treasures to be grateful for. Don't stop what you've been doing well. Hold on to what you've learned from your family and friends. Let the great experiences of your DTS enrich what you've already been doing and add a sprinkling of flavour to the community you are part of.

Others of you who are reading this book have made a lot of changes during DTS. Life at home was and is very different from what you experienced in YWAM. You may feel pulled, torn, and confused between these ways of life. It's not easy to go back and forth between such different worlds. You may experience uncomfortable tensions and friction. The challenge you face is of deciding which aspects of DTS life you will hold on to. You may have to do this while *unlearning* certain habits, patterns, and assumptions.

This was the challenge I faced after graduating from DTS. My life changed dramatically in DTS, and upon my return home from YWAM, I had to find a faith community, role models, friends, and activities that helped me grow in my faith. I had to re-evaluate the music I listened to, the shows I watched, my vocabulary, the books I read, what I did for fun, and who I turned to for advice. It was not easy.

However, God helped me to adjust and transition. With His help, I made the decisions I needed to and took small steps forward. I trust He will help you as well.

No matter where you've come from or what lies ahead of you, you were not designed to live a life of faith alone. You may be far away from people who have helped you grow in God, but you do not have to stay isolated. This devotional book isn't going to tell you what to do next, but it's a tool to help you stay connected to God and to strengthen your community of relationships.

Each week, from Monday to Saturday, you will read a devotion I've written with you in mind. Each devotion includes questions and activities to help you process the material and integrate your DTS experience. On Sunday, you'll take a break from the devotions and will get the chance to review last week and plan for the week to come.

On devotional days, you'll read a passage from the gospel of Mark. If you can, use a hardcopy Bible. Get a journal and pen and find a place where you can be undisturbed. Read the passage slowly, once or twice. Let the routine of opening this book, quieting your heart, and shifting your attention to God become a daily routine. In DTS you developed new habits connected to prayer, Bible reading, and worship. Let going through this devotional book become a habit for this season of re-entry.

Each devotion includes a short reflection, questions to think about, action steps, and suggestions for going deeper. Don't worry about trying to answer every question or take every action step. Go as deep as you like with the time and energy you have. Go through the devotion at whatever time of day works best for you: morning, lunch, after work, before bed.

On the seventh day of the week, you'll do a *Sunday reflection*. The questions and activities for this day are to help you reflect on the past week. You'll look at the interactions, activities, and experiences of the past week, think about how you are doing physically, emotionally, and spiritually, and pay attention to what God might be saying to you. Then you'll have the chance to look at the coming week and set goals for what you want to accomplish.

Time to Leave the Greenhouse

I once heard a pastor talk about ways DTS is a type of *greenhouse* for Christian growth. Greenhouses are artificial structures designed to protect tender plants from cold, strong winds, destructive predators, and more. The environment inside a greenhouse is carefully monitored to maximize growth and boost fruitfulness.

The environment inside a YWAM training centre is closely designed and monitored as well. Students are shielded from danger, and risks are limited. Each activity and assignment is planned to help students grow, build trust, become stronger in God, learn healthy ways of relating, take steps of surrender, and so on. A lot of growth can happen in a greenhouse.

However, there is a limit to how much plants can grow in the greenhouse. Staying inside for too long can actually hinder growth. Living things were meant to flourish in the big, wide world. They need to experience the pressures of the wind, the variety in temperatures, and the changes of the seasons in order to build strength.

So, at some point (and often sooner than we wanted) the DTS ended, and it was time to leave the greenhouse. The transition from life inside to life outside can be shocking! Beautiful plants that had been fed, watered, and protected now have to learn how to feed and protect themselves.

The debrief and re-entry teaching in DTS gave you tools for this transition. The notes from these teachings are a great resource for days you experience the shock of life outside the greenhouse. Realize, however, there's no way to avoid the turbulence of transition. Knowing what to expect is better than not knowing at all, but notes from a lecture and books about re-entry (including this one) can't take away all the pain, frustration, or confusion.

You have lived outside the greenhouse before, and you can do so again. Life outside is full of opportunities, not only challenges or dangers. God is with you! He has called you, sent you, and led you to *this* place. Try to look at each re-entry shock you experience as a reminder of the amazing things you experienced in your DTS. Maybe there's a way for you to take what you've experienced and create them for others to enjoy. Maybe you'll return to another greenhouse in the future for another season of development and training.

But for now, what parts of life in the greenhouse helped you the most? Which of the structures and supports from the greenhouse aren't needed anymore? Which of the pressures and challenges outside the greenhouse can help you grow and become stronger? Where can you go for the help and support you need when the stormy winds start blowing and you want to return to the greenhouse?

These are some of the questions we'll look at over the next ten weeks together, so keep them in mind as we look to the life of Jesus in the Gospel of Mark.

Week One

Day 1 - Beginnings—Exciting and Scary!

Read: Mark 1:1-8

Reflection:

BEGINNINGS ARE USUALLY EXCITING and exhilarating. A new sketch pad, the opening credits to a movie, cracking the spine of a book, unwrapping a package from Amazon. Anticipation of something wonderful to come can be a very strong motivator. There are many mornings when the hope of coffee is what gets me out of bed!

When John the Baptist spoke in the wilderness, people thronged to hear what he had to say. The crowds were looking for something new, something to put their hope in, something that would improve their lives. John didn't speak of a thing that was coming, but of a person—someone who was worth waiting for, a mighty one, promised and sent by God Himself! At the time, John didn't even know who he was talking about, but he trusted in God's promises and was making space in his life for the promised Messiah.

You may remember the excitement of beginning DTS. New suitcase, new people, and new adventures. You probably came to DTS with hopes and expectations that God would do good things in you and through you. I hope your expectations were met or even surpassed. However, DTS is over now, and you may or may not be happy about that.

And even while you are trying to make sense of the past months, you have already begun another new phase of life. Re-entry. Transition. Life after DTS! Mixed in with the sadness of saying goodbye to DTS friends and the joy of seeing family and loved ones again, you may have questions, fears, and hopes for the season ahead.

What is God going to do?

How can I be sure to make the right decision?

Will I have to wait long to see what He has for me next?

John the Baptist invited people to a new way of living: to leave behind the old and walk into something different. He spoke about repentance and forgiveness. He recalled God's promises and stirred up hope. He spoke about the Coming One who would show them the way.

Like so many in the crowd in the wilderness, you have already said *yes* to this life. You have said *yes* to following the One John spoke about. You have traded your old life for a new life. Today is a day to walk in hope and courage, knowing the Promised One is with you, and knowing that there are more good things to come.

Something to Think About:

1. In your opinion, what is it about beginnings that make them so exciting?
2. What were some of your hopes on the day you began your DTS?
3. What were some of the fears you experienced as you started DTS?

Action Steps:

1. Remember how and when you heard the invitation to leave behind the "old life" and begin a new life with God. What was that experience like?
2. If you only had two or three minutes to tell a friend about your "new life" with Jesus, what would you say?

Going Deeper:

1. Write a message or call someone who played a part in the beginning of your "new life" in God. Thank him/her for taking the time to be a part of how you met Jesus.
2. Would you describe yourself as more of a "starter" or a "finisher"? What are the strengths

and weaknesses of how you are wired in this regard?

3. What do you sense God is inviting you to for this next season? What are some possible steps you could take to explore that direction?

Day 2 - Before He Did Anything Amazing

Read: Mark 1:9-13

Reflection:

Highs and lows are an unavoidable part of life, right? Life's not always a bowl of cherries. What goes up must come down. Gravity. Entropy. All that stuff.

At His baptism, Jesus had the type of encounter with the Father I have always dreamed of. Imagine it: a voice from heaven, crystal clear affirmation of God's approval, a physical sign of His love and acceptance. Must have been amazing!

But then, in no time, Jesus is heading straight into the wilderness for a head-to-head with the devil. The joy and excitement of that sunny day at the Jordan River fade away and are replaced by gnawing hunger, bitter loneliness, and perhaps moments of despair.

During those days in the wilderness, Jesus must have wondered: *How will I survive this temptation? Isn't there an easier way? What did I do wrong?*

What touches me most as I read this account in Jesus' life is the realization that the Father declared His love and approval of Jesus *before* Jesus endured extreme temptation, did any fancy miracles, or preached any profound sermons.

Back at home, with the highs of DTS fresh in our memory, it can be tempting to think our approval and worth comes from what we have done or will accomplish *for God.* Now that DTS is over and life is back to normal, it's easy to wonder how the Father feels about us when we aren't doing amazing things for Him.

When I start to question if the Father is pleased with me or not—when I find myself thinking about what I should to do to *prove* my faith is alive and strong—I have to stop myself. Being part of the family of God puts us on the same footing as Jesus himself. We are God's sons and daughters. He loves us, and He delights in us. We don't have to try to prove we are worthy of His love. He's already declared that we are!

Something to Think About:

1. What is the significance of the Father proclaiming His approval and love of Jesus before any of Jesus' miracles or signs?
2. How easy (or difficult) is it for you to believe you are beloved in God's sight on the low days, as well as during the highlight moments?
3. Are there things you find yourself doing in an effort to gain God's love or approval? If so, invite God to meet you in that place and remind you of His acceptance and love.

Action Steps:

1. What kinds of highs and lows did you experience in your DTS? List five highs and five lows from the past five or six months of your life.
2. Ask the Holy Spirit to show you what the Father thinks about you. Ask the Father this question, and then spend five minutes journaling His response.
3. Write a note of affirmation to someone in your life and send it to them. Proclaim the truth of who he/she is as a person, not just what he/she does for you or others.

Going Deeper:

1. Choose a Scripture verse that proclaims your value to God. Write it out and post it somewhere you can see it each day.

Day 3 - The Courage to Follow

Read: Mark 1:14-20

Reflection:

Follow Me.

How did that invitation sound to the fishermen listening to Jesus on the beach that day?

Everybody had heard about John the Baptizer's capture and knew he was sitting in prison. His bold declarations had upset some very powerful people. Now the jailbird's relative, Jesus, is inviting fishermen to join Him in what He's doing. He asks these regular, working men to toss aside the security of their life and follow Him to the unknown.

What did this invitation mean for these men? What risks and cost came with saying "yes" to Jesus? If they agreed to follow the man from Nazareth, would they be the next ones thrown in jail?

However, in spite of the risks, these men were willing. With many unanswered questions still in mind and with all the fears before them, Simon, Andrew, James, and John left their nets and homes to follow Jesus. I don't automatically think of fishermen as possessing extraordinary bravery or faith, but their courage is surprising.

You are a person of courage, too. Attending a DTS was full of risk and of unknowns. In response to the call of Jesus, you left people and opportunities behind, and you followed Him. You have endured the challenges and tests, and you have grown in significant ways. And now that DTS is finished, you want to continue to follow where He leads you. Good on you!

It may not be clear what Jesus is calling you to next. Maybe you have an idea about studying, getting involved in your church, returning as a YWAM staffer, or getting more training. Maybe it's not clear to you at all yet.

Take heart and know that you are in good company. For

thousands of years, normal people like you and me—fishermen, teenagers, students, the poor, the wealthy, the dedicated, and the confused—have been responding to Jesus' invitation to "follow Me." He knows what He's doing. He knows how to lead, and He wants to live life with you.

Let's trust Him to lead us, and let's keep our eyes on Him.

Something to Think About:

1. How have you seen Jesus' leading in your life so far? What's an example of a time you responded to His invitation to *follow Him*?
2. Looking back on your decision to attend DTS, what do you notice about the way God led you in making that decision?
3. What are some of the fears or unknowns you are facing right now? Write them in a journal or notebook.

Action Steps:

1. Make a list of all the ways you are following Jesus right now. This could be as simple as loving your enemy (or an "ex" you haven't seen in six months); forgiving someone who hurt your feelings yesterday (like your sister or best friend); being generous to others (a parent or coworker); or giving your worries to Jesus. When you do the things Jesus asks you to do, you *are* following Him!
2. Set up a time to Skype or chat with a DTS friend

a staff member (or someone else) about "an unknown" you are facing. Though you may be far in distance from your classmates, you are *not* alone. God has given you a community of people who love you, so keep sharing your life with people who care about you.

3. Spend some time with God reflecting on the fears or unknowns you wrote down in Question 3 above. As best as you can, cast these cares on the Lord, remembering His love for you and His promise to be with you always.

Going Deeper:

1. Jesus said *follow Me* over twenty times in the gospels. Do you see this as a command, an invitation, a suggestion, or a mixture of them all? What's the difference between a command, an invitation, and a suggestion? Take some time to journal your answer.
2. Use a Bible program to search all the times Jesus says *follow Me*. How do people respond to these words from Him? What can you learn from their responses?

Day 4 - Getting Some Stories of My Own

Read: Mark 1:21-28

Reflection:

There was *something* remarkable about Jesus. Something about the way He spoke and interacted with people. He was different from the religious leaders of His day who quoted ancient scholars, recited boring speeches, and tried to sound impressive. When Jesus spoke, people wanted to listen. When He talked about God, He sounded like He knew what He was talking about. He had authority because He had experience with the Father.

Years ago, after I'd been in YWAM for eight years, I came to a crossroads of sorts. I knew I loved missions and being in YWAM. I loved hearing cool testimonies and telling them to others. I wanted to teach and mobilize. In a moment of clarity, I realized most of the anecdotes I was telling were the experiences of other people. I was passing on second-hand material. It was great to learn about God's character and ways from those around me, but I was hungry for the opportunity to live my own stories.

I realized I had to get out of my comfort zone and stop living on second-hand stories. I made a decision to place myself somewhere that would stretch me, a place where I could see and experience His works firsthand.

This desire propelled me to move to Central Asia for a year. After the year was over, I had grown into a new level of confidence. I had overcome challenges and had grown as a teacher, a worker, and a follower of Jesus. I ended up going back to the same place for three more years, immersing myself in another language and culture. I was surrounded by people who were both curious and suspicious about Jesus and my faith. Some days it seemed so much harder to live a good story than to simply read one from a book. But as the months went by, and through plenty of successes and failures, I was able to be part of some really cool God stories.

Those stories are mine now, and it feels good to have them.

Something to Think About:

1. You have come back from an intense 5-6 months of growing in your relationship with God. How would you say you have grown in your authority as a follower of Christ?
2. If you could ask your friends and family about the ways you changed during DTS, what do you think they would say?
3. What are some specific areas where you have gained authority through obedience, confession, repentance, prayer, etc.?

Action Steps:

1. What are some of the most significant encounters you had with Jesus during DTS? Think through the weeks of lecture phase and outreach, and make a list of significant memories.
2. What areas in your personal life or your walk with God would you like to develop? Spend some time thinking, praying, or journaling about this.

Going Deeper:

1. Ask a classmate from DTS how they saw you change during the DTS. Let that person know what growth you saw in him/her as well.
2. Read 1 Corinthians 12 and 13. What does Paul say about desiring spiritual gifts? What is the connection between the gifts and love?

Day 5 - Jesus Didn't Have Office Hours

Read: Mark 1:29-34

Reflection:

When evening had come, after the sun had set, people brought the sick and evil-afflicted people to Jesus (v. 32).

Imagine the work day is over. Most people are relaxing at home, putting up their feet, and enjoying the end of a long day.

For Jesus, though, and for those in need of His help, this particular evening has a very different agenda. There is action and movement. There is work still to be done. There are knocks on the door. Pleas for help. People come in sick and leave healthy! Those who are frustrated and in pain, longing for a miracle, have their needs met by this man, Jesus.

I like how Jesus didn't post office hours on the door of the homes where He stayed. Whenever someone came to Jesus, He made time for them.

He doesn't have office hours now, either. He doesn't shut the door in my face and say, "Come back tomorrow. I'm tired and done for the day."

He is always available.

He is limitless in energy and compassion.

He doesn't yawn, and His mind doesn't wander while I'm talking.

He is attentive and engaged.

He knows what I need. He clearly sees what's going on with me.

One of the difficult adjustments to life after DTS is finding time to see people you care about. During DTS, you were with your teammates and staff 24/7. It was easy to find someone to talk with, pray with, or hang out with. But now, back home, people are busy. Coffees and prayer meetings and games of Frisbee have to be scheduled and planned. You may feel neglected or low on the list of priorities.

If this is the case for you, try to be patient with your friends and family. They had to adjust to you being away, and they will adjust to you being back. Don't give up easily. Keep asking to hang out, and keep showing up. Be the kind of friend to others you would like to have yourself.

And, like it says in the reading: when everything around is dark, when everyone else is busy, and when you don't know where to turn, Jesus can give you His attention and bring hope to all of the places where you need it.

Something to Think About:

1. What are the areas in your life that seem dark or unclear right now?
2. If you were standing at the door to Simon and Andrew's house, waiting to see Jesus, what would you ask Him for?
3. What has it been like to adjust to the pace and schedule of life back home? Are you happy with how busy you are?

Action Steps:

1. Are there any people in your life who might need help right now—a listening ear, someone who is safe? Think of three people who currently need healing, help, or encouragement. Contact them to see if they would like to get together, or if you could *bring them to Jesus* by praying for them.
2. Consider the people in your life you want to spend time with during this season. How can you be intentional to schedule time with them, or make sure you see them on a regular basis? If you haven't done so already, contact them to let them know you want to hang out.

Going Deeper:

1. Take the opportunity to pray for the "country of the day" (or a country that you are interested in) by looking at the Operation World website, operationworld.org.
2. For a great resource to help you be focused and intentional each day, check out Donald Miller's *Storyline Productivity Schedule* by visiting storylineblog.com and searching "storyline productivity schedule." There's no magic formula in this document, but it has helped me identify goals and priorities for each day. In times of transition and change, it can be nice to have a bit of structure in this regard.
3. No *person* on earth is limitless in love, energy, or time like God is. Sometimes we put expectations on people that only God can live up to. At other times, we approach God like He's a moody friend or a forgetful grandparent. It's easy to be disappointed or confused when we expect people to be like God, or when we expect God to be like people! Take time to talk with God about what it means that He is limitless in love and goodness, that His power is greater than any other, and that He is the smartest being of all. See what He might share with you about who He is and what this means for you today.

Day 6 - Waking Up Before Your Alarm

Read: Mark 1:35-39

Reflection:

Have you had the wonderful experience of waking up before your alarm goes off, feeling full of energy and ready to start the day? Though I consider myself a morning person, this doesn't happen to me very often. So when it does happen, I savour it.

One of the things I respect the most about Jesus is the way He lived with such energy and purpose. He didn't need deadlines or reminders to stay focused on the tasks before Him. He was up early, meeting with His Father, ready to visit villages, to teach crowds, or to cast out demons. He greeted the day like a little kid on Christmas morning—every morning!

Somehow Jesus found a way to stay on track, motivated, and energized to do the things He knew were important. When I read the Gospels, I feel tired just thinking of His schedule and day-to-day life. Yet I don't get the impression He was forced or guilted into the things He did. His actions don't seem dutiful; they seem passionate, full of conviction and inner drive.

His self-leadership and initiative impress me. I wonder where He got all his determination and energy. His ongoing connection with the Father was a significant source of energy and strength, for sure. His friendships with others, the satisfaction of helping so many, and the inner joy of offering His life to God as an act of worship must have been other motivators for Him.

As a human, Jesus would have experienced all the ups and downs that you and I experience. He knows what it's like to be welcomed and rejected. He understands how it feels to be respected for what you've been doing, and what it's like to be looked down upon for your choices. He offered His gifts and talents to people who were eager to hear what He said, and He was also run out of town by angry crowds of people.

Coming home from DTS can be a mixed bag of emotions, responses from others, and ideas about what's next. Don't be surprised if you find yourself on a roller coaster of emotional highs and lows. What might be stranger is if you *didn't* have strong feelings about what you've experienced or what you anticipate next.

As we look to Jesus as our example of how to live well, it's worth thinking about His daily life. He had a clear picture of "what I came for" (v. 38), and it kept Him going even in the difficult times. How can we get the same focus and motivation for our life as He had for His? How can we find the same energy to keep going each day, regardless of the ups and downs we might face?

Something to Think About:

1. Think about which things in your daily life help you connect to the Father and get charged up for all the things you do. How can you stay charged and refueled, especially in this time of transition and change?

2. List three specific times in DTS when you felt connected to God. What were you doing when you felt this connected?
3. How do your schedule and daily habits now compare to a normal day during DTS? Is there anything you'd like to change or adjust?

Action Steps:

1. Choose one thing you would get out of bed early to do this week: coffee with a friend, going for a hike, watching a favorite movie, Skyping with a DTS classmate, etc. How can you make that idea a reality this week? Plan to do it.
2. Make a list of the things/people/activities in your life that drain you or sap your energy. What could you do in response to this list?
3. At what time of day do you feel the most energized and inspired? Consider being intentional to spend some of that part of the day with Jesus at least once this week.

Going Deeper:

1. A book I've enjoyed over the years is *Wild at Heart* by John Eldredge. In it he writes a lot about the importance of discovering what stirs you at the deepest level. A favorite quote from the book is, "Don't ask yourself what the world needs, ask yourself what makes you come alive, because what the world needs is people who have come alive."

Spend some time thinking about what it is that makes you come alive.

Day 7 - Sunday Reflection

Welcome to Sunday. By this time you've read six devotionals and have had a week to think about your DTS experience. You've been looking at the life and ministry of Jesus, reflecting on how He was loved by the Father. You've seen Him call people to follow Him, begin to heal the sick, and you've seen some of the creative ways He stays connected to the Father.

Even as you've been thinking about these things, you've been hanging out with friends and family, missing your classmates, trying to be present where you are now, but realizing that pieces of your heart have spread all over the world. People are probably asking you, "What are you going to do now?" and "How are you planning to pay for that?" These questions can provoke excitement and fear, and there's a lot of pressure to know the answers right now!

I'd like to invite you to take a break from these pressures. You don't have to come up with a life plan today. Sometimes we think growth has to happen quickly and dramatically. We believe the more important a task or goal is, the less time there is for rest. This thinking is a bit backward. Healthy growth *always* requires rest.

So today we're taking a break from a daily devotion. In its place, you are invited to think about the past week and to consider your plans for the week ahead. You may find it helpful to write down your experiences from the past week and your goals for next week. Keeping track of what you've done, what you aim to do, and noticing any gaps between the two can help you see patterns in your life. Be open to what God may want to speak to you through this process.

This is totally optional, by the way. You might find that what you really need is to take a complete break from this book! Maybe today you decide to go for a long walk instead. Everyone is different; for some of us (like me), reviewing the past week and planning for the week ahead is relaxing. For others, it's stressful. These Sabbath reviews are offered each Sunday if you feel the desire for more structured reflection, but feel free to skip them if they defeat the purpose of the Sabbath for you!

Sabbath Review: Week One

Take twenty to thirty minutes at some point today to look back over the past week and plan for the next, considering the following categories:

1. Connection. In the past week, who have you connected with? Think about family members, roommates, friends from DTS, people at church, work or school friends. How did you feel about the quality of the time you spent together? How well did you listen? Is there anything that could have made the time together better?

For the coming week, consider making an appointment to connect with your pastor or youth pastor. Tell them about what God did in your life during DTS, and ask about what needs the church currently has.

2. Service and Generosity. In what ways have you

expressed a heart of service and generosity this week? Being willing to serve is a great way to express gratitude and love to others. Service and generosity can look like washing the dishes, taking out the garbage, giving someone a ride somewhere, or asking someone about their day and listening with your full attention. Service and generosity can look like colouring with a child, calling your grandma to say "hello," letting someone ahead of you in the grocery line, or letting someone else decide which movie to watch.

For the coming week, consider how and whom you can serve. Service and generosity can't always be scheduled. Instead they can flow as a response to the people and situations around you. However, it can be easy to get so scheduled and busy you have no time left to help others. Are there opportunities at your church, in your neighbourhood, or with your extended family? Ask God to open your eyes to the needs (spoken and unspoken) around you and to keep your heart tender and willing to respond.

3. Self-care. How have you been taking care of yourself this week? Have you been getting enough sleep? Are you eating well? Are you drinking enough water? What are you doing for exercise? Have you made time for "play," for things you find truly enjoyable: things so fun for you that you lose track of time when doing them? (This could be reading, sports, crafting, hanging out with friends, you name it.)

For the coming week, maybe you make a doctor's appointment to attend to any health concerns that arose during DTS. See if you can set aside time for a hobby or a fun outing, too.

4. Spiritual Life. In what ways have you been able to connect with God this week? Where have you sensed His presence as you go about your daily life? Which habits (such as reading Scripture, worship, prayer, Bible study, etc.) have you been able to engage in? What do you sense God is saying to you these days? In what ways do you sense His encouragement and affirmation of you as His child?

For the coming week, how and when can you make time to connect with God? Consider what you've discovered about yourself regarding the time of day and type of setting you are most alert and able to focus on God.

Week Two

Day 8 - He is Both Willing and Able

Read: Mark 1:40-45

Reflection:

WHEN FACED with a problem that's too big to solve on my own, I mentally go through a list of people with the *ability* to help me and the *willingness* to help me. To get assistance with solving my problem, it's important to have both qualities in the same person. If someone wants to help but doesn't know what they're doing, the situation might end up worse than before! I've learned to ask my brother for tech help because he knows his stuff *and* he's willing to use these skills to help me—even at strange hours of the night.

The leper's healing is one of the first miracles we read

about in the gospel of Mark. Those who witnessed the words and actions of Jesus were often shocked by what He said and did. They debated where His power came from and questioned the signs He performed. But this leper was as confident as could be that Jesus had what it took to heal him. He boldly informed Jesus, "You can heal me, if you are willing." The healing part he was sure of. What he wasn't sure of was Jesus' *willingness* to help him.

In this story we see two significant aspects of the nature and character of God. Jesus displays both the *power* of God to heal the leper and the *willingness* of God to respond to his need.

In DTS you learned about and experienced attributes of God's nature and character. You studied His power, strength, wisdom, and ability. You heard about His kindness, care, love, and concern for you. But now, back home, it can be challenging to keep on asking for His help and to keep on trusting Him, especially when you have to wait for answers.

I've often wished for the confidence of this leper. I know I *should* believe God is willing and able to help me, but at times I find myself fearful and timid. I get stuck in my uncertainty. I wonder if God has become tired of helping me. Maybe my request is too silly. Maybe He's got other things on His mind. Maybe He's annoyed I can't find a solution on my own.

If you're feeling any of these things, let's go back to the example of the leper in this story. Let's hold on to what we've heard and learned about Jesus. Let's present ourselves and our needs to God, remembering His love *and* His power. We can't make God give us what we ask for, but we can come to Him, confident He hears and cares for us: and that's a pretty great place to be.

Something to Think About:

1. Which of these is harder for you to wrap your mind around: The idea that God is *able* to help you, or the idea that God is *willing* to help you? Where might these ideas have come from?
2. What are some recent examples of times when you asked God for help with something but didn't see the answer or results you were hoping for? How did you feel in these situations?

Action Steps:

1. Take five minutes to reflect on the concerns or burdens that are weighing you down at the moment. Don't gloss over what's bothering you or pretend you feel differently than you do. Imagine yourself coming to Jesus, just as the leper came before Him. What would you say to Jesus? What would you ask Him to help you with? Imagine Him reaching out His hand to touch you, just as He touched the leper. Listen to what He might speak to your heart in response to your requests.
2. Read through a few of your favourite Psalms. Pay attention to what the writer seems to understand about God's power/ability and His willingness/love. What similarities do you notice about the writer and your own views of God?

What differences do you see between the writer and yourself?

Going Deeper:

1. In this passage we read how the leper fell to his knees in front of Jesus, asking to be healed. This is a powerful image and speaks about the desperation and humility of the leper. What is your most common "posture" in prayer? In worship? Think about different postures you could take as you draw near to God. How could these different postures help you to express your heart to God?
2. One of my favourite Bible verses is Hebrews 10:23, "*Let us hold fast the confession of our hope without wavering, for He who promised is faithful.*" Holding fast to what we've learned about God takes practice. Take some time to read and meditate on Hebrews 10:19-25. What can you learn from these verses about how to hold on to hope? What role do others play in helping us stay connected to God and aware of His presence in our life?

Day 9 - Friends Who Carry Each Other

Read: Mark 2:1-12

Reflection:

If you've watched the third *Lord of the Rings* movie, *The Return of the King,* you might be able to see the connection between the four men lowering their friend through the ceiling to Jesus and the scene where Sam picks up Frodo and carries him. In both cases, the friends in the story realize they are limited in what they can do to help, but they aren't willing to give up easily. Big challenges call for creative solutions. The paralyzed man's friends can't heal him, and Sam can't carry the Ring, but in both cases the friends are willing to put great effort into doing what they can.

In this passage, the paralyzed man's friends found a solution for getting their friend to Jesus. When the crowds of people blocked their way, they didn't give up. Convinced Jesus could do something for their friend, they "creatively" removed the barriers that stood between him and Jesus.

Do you have friends like this? Friends who would carry you when the situation was desperate? Friends who would lower you through a roof if needed?

I hope you experienced deep friendships during your DTS. I'd had friends before DTS—good friends—but during DTS I learned what it was like to include God in my friendships. Having God in my life changed the way I was able to love my friends.

I was deeply impacted by the quality and depth of friendship I experienced in DTS. People who were complete strangers a few weeks before would pray with me about areas of deep concern until late at night. I was given extravagant gifts. People I was just getting to know extended forgiveness toward me. Roommates and staff patiently bore with my rudeness, anger, and irritating habits. They did so with smiles and joy, never giving the impression I was a project, a burden, or a waste of their time.

Many people live their entire lives without friends like this. Some people don't realize sacrificial love is one of the treasures of deep friendships, and many are afraid to ask for or offer help to the degree we read about in the Scripture passage.

Extravagant love finds its source in Jesus—and He is able to help us love others with a love beyond what we could ever deserve, or offer. Let's continue to learn from Him, and one another, about what love looks like. Let's invest our time and energy in deep friendships and trust God to help us along the way.

Something to Think About:

1. How would you describe yourself as a friend?
2. When and in what ways have you been "an extravagant friend" to others?
3. Which of your friends have taught you the most about friendship? What did you learn from them, and how can you apply this in your current relationships?

Action Steps:

1. Who are the people in your life you could "carry to Jesus" in prayer right now? Ask Holy Spirit to show you how to pray for the people around you.

If it helps, imagine making a hole in the roof and lowering these people down to Jesus's waiting arms.

2. On a global scale, what are three issues or areas of concern (trafficking, poverty, domestic violence, bullying, refugees) that continue to get your attention? Set a reminder on your phone right now to take five minutes each day for the next week to pray about these issues.

Going Deeper:

1. Read Isaiah 61:1-3. God's Spirit wants to use us to bring transformation to the world. Make a list of the verbs (action words) in this passage. What can you learn from this passage about the kinds of things God would ask you to be doing?
2. Check out the YouTube video, "Are you a trader," by 4545Drew.
3. Watch *The Return of the King*. How does this film inspire you in regard to friendship?

Day 10 - The Power of an Invitation

Read: Mark 2:13-17

Reflection:

What a funny scene this is! Picture it with me: Jesus and His disciples strolling by the lake, shooting the breeze, enjoying the sunshine. Out of the blue, Jesus spots Levi at work, up to his ears in paperwork and financial reports. Without introductory chitchat or an apology for the interruption, Jesus invites Levi to follow Him. Even more surprising is that, without even blinking an eye (it would seem), Levi stands up, abandons his tax booth, and follows Jesus. Who would have guessed?

When I was in school, I didn't get many invitations. I wasn't popular. I didn't have people lining up to talk with me or inviting me to join their adventures. I had daydreams of excitement and adventure, of meeting mysterious strangers, or of talking with someone famous. However, my daydreams remained only that. But for Levi, this was his day! As he walked to work that morning, did he have any idea about the invitation he would receive or where it would lead him?

Of all the people to be invited to join Jesus on His mission, Levi seemed an unlikely choice. Yet Jesus understood there is always more to a person than what first meets the eye. It's tempting to look at person's career, clothing, hobbies, or opinions and think we know everything about them. It's easy to judge people and disqualify them before even giving them a chance. Could it be that the bored and directionless, the confused and obnoxious, or even the ones with questionable character traits, are the exact ones most in need of an invitation to something different?

Levi's career as a tax collector didn't disqualify him from

being invited to be with Jesus. Aren't you glad your past didn't disqualify you either?

Something to Think About:

1. Explain in your own words what you think Jesus meant by the statement, "I did not come to call the righteous, but sinners."
2. What are the things in your past, or in your life today, that you fear may disqualify you from being used by God? What does He think about those things?

Action Steps:

1. An invitation is a powerful thing. It communicates interest, value, and friendship. There is always the risk an invitation will be rejected, but many great things have come from the simple question: "Do you want to come with me?" Are there people you could "invite" in some way? Take a few moments to ask Holy Spirit. Write down what you are going to do about it.
2. Think of someone in your life who saw potential in you and invited you to a different type of living or relating. Contact him/her to say thank you.
3. Are there any habits, beliefs, prejudices, or relationships in your life Jesus might be inviting you to leave behind in order to follow Him? Take a moment and invite Holy Spirit to search your heart. If something comes to mind, commit to confessing this to someone you trust. Pray with

this person for the ability to surrender this and walk in greater freedom.

Going Deeper:

1. Donald Miller's *A Million Miles in a Thousand Years* is a thought-provoking book about what it means to be the hero in your own life story: how to know what you want, and how to overcome obstacles in your path. I highly recommend it!
2. When you have 30 minutes to be inspired about how our lives can impact others, watch this amazing documentary, *Godspeed: The Pace of Being Known.* You can find it at livegodspeed.org. "Follow the story of an American pastor whose desire to change the world grinds to a halt in a Scottish parish."

Day 11 - Judgment Never Gives You What You Really Want

Read: Mark 2:18-28

Reflection:

Judging another person's actions and choices is incredibly easy. It's also one of the quickest ways to feel better about yourself. You can judge people in any location, at any time of the day or night, without lifting a finger. It doesn't cost you anything.

Evaluating and judging (and condemning) is as common in our culture as it was in Jesus' day. The world is full of people who are making bad decisions. You don't have to look that hard before you can find someone doing worse off than you. When I say to myself, "I'm more together than she is," or "I'm more spiritual than him," or "At least I don't waste my money like that!" I can feel good for a little while. But it never lasts long. In the long run, that kind of comparison never gets me what I want.

What comparison does is shine a spotlight on my exact area of insecurity. I'm never more judgmental than when I feel unloved, untalented, and fearful. It's especially easy to judge when I'm outside of my comfort zone and am looking for secure footing in new territory.

In the early days of my DTS, I made my share of judgments and evaluations of the people around me. There were lots of things to pick at and criticize. Different cultures and accents, different denominations and habits. Different personalities and ideas. But what was different about the DTS setting was that I had the opportunity to get to know each person I'd been judging. No longer anonymous strangers, I soon discovered we each had a story to tell. We were all carrying pain and wounds and hopes. We were in it together, and that was amazing!

Before long, I was able to see the value of each person. I felt accepted and safe, and there wasn't the same need to worry about how we all measured up. We had places to go and a world to change! As we shared life together, it became easier and easier to let go of judgment and comparison.

But now, after DTS, life gets complicated once again. Yes, there are some people you know well, but each day there are new relationships to navigate: work, school, church. Things have changed while you've been gone. You've changed. People may have new expectations—or they may expect you to be the same as you were before. No matter how you slice it, this is a time in life where there are many reasons to feel insecure, confused, nervous, or afraid. It's easy to resort to a posture of comparison and judgment.

Beware of giving in to the easy confidence booster: judgment. It won't take you where you want to go. In truth, a person can feel it when we're being judged and measured, and nobody likes that feeling.

You are infinitely valuable to Jesus. He can fill you up with love and affirmation as often as needed. When you need to be reminded of where you stand and how loved you are, go to Him. He's got plenty of good things to say to you.

Something to Think About:

1. Think about the way your relationship with people at DTS changed over time. Can you relate to what I've written about evaluating people when you first meet them, but then learning to give grace to others when you know their story? Why do you think that is?
2. What kinds of things have you noticed yourself judging or criticizing since you've returned home?
3. Have you been comparing yourself to others—people from DTS, or people back at home? Where has this comparison taken you?

Action Steps:

1. The Pharisees questioned Jesus and His disciples about their lifestyle. There may be people who are questioning your life now—especially if you changed while you were at DTS. How can you respond to these questions in a loving way?
2. What are the changes you want to keep up with from DTS (in speech, habits, or activities)? Consider what it will look like to hold on to these changes.
3. Write down some "advice to self" about what you learned and experienced at DTS. This advice could be anything: listen to worship music in the car, write in a journal regularly, keep a daily gratitude list, ask for prayer, etc. Put the advice somewhere you will be able to see it.

Going Deeper:

1. Make an effort to build relationship with someone in your life you find easy to judge, or someone you don't know well. See what you can learn about their story. Go for coffee or lunch with them. Be open about your own story as well.
2. For a great book to get you thinking about the way judgment and criticism rob us of love and freedom, check out *Repenting of Religion* by Greg Boyd.

Day 12 - Simply Do What Is Good

Read: Mark 3:1-6

Reflection:

Everyone was watching Jesus. He was so interesting—always saying and doing surprising things. You could never predict what He would do next, but you could be sure it would be worth talking about.

The religious leaders were always testing Him—watching for Him to make a mistake, looking for something to criticize—trying to make Him look bad so they could look better. It's a familiar story, isn't it?

Jesus' response to the tests and judgment of the religious leaders was simply to do what was good. He saw the man with a withered hand, had compassion on him, and used His power to do good. He refused to be intimidated by what people *might* say or how they *might* criticize Him. I'm so impressed by that!

Now that you're home from DTS, a missionary fresh off the field, it's possible people are looking at you: wondering if you have changed, wondering how you are going to live. Some people will be happy about the changes they see; others will be suspicious or critical.

The choice before you is how will you respond to those around you: people who put you on a spiritual pedestal, ones who question your choices, those who only talk about themselves? Some may insult and criticize your faith, wondering what happened to the "old" you.

While it might seem like a good idea to show people how much you've learned by starting debates about theology, bragging about travel stories, or trying to "out-pray" them, don't be distracted by these things. Follow the example of Jesus to simply do what is good. Let goodness, kindness, patience, faith, and peace win out over all the things that might come against you.

Something to Think About:

1. Are there any situations right now where you feel criticized, judged, or as though people are waiting for you to make a mistake? How do you usually respond in situations like that? Is there anything you'd like to do differently in the future?
2. Are there any situations right now where you know what you're supposed to do, but you're afraid of what others might think?
3. On a scale of one to ten, how much do you struggle with fear of man?
4. Who in your life is a role model for you of someone who does what's right, even when it hurts?

Action Steps:

1. Write out Philippians 4:8 and put it somewhere you can see. What is the connection between the things we think about and God's promise to us?
2. Write out the list of the fruits of the Spirit from Galatians 5:22-23. Which ones in the list are the easiest for you? Which ones are difficult? Is there

anything Jesus wants to say to you about this? Spend some time listening to Him.

Going Deeper:

1. Reflect on these words by Mother Teresa:

"People are often unreasonable, irrational, and self-centered.

Forgive them anyway.

If you are kind, people may accuse you of selfish, ulterior motives.

Be kind anyway.

If you are successful, you will win some unfaithful friends and some genuine enemies.

Succeed anyway.

If you are honest and sincere people may deceive you.

Be honest and sincere anyway.

What you spend years creating, others could destroy overnight.

Create anyway.

If you find serenity and happiness, some may be jealous.

Be happy anyway.

> The good you do today, will often be forgotten.
>
> Do good anyway.
>
> Give the best you have, and it will never be enough.
>
> Give your best anyway.
>
> You see, in the final analysis, it is between you and God.
>
> It was never between you and them anyway."

Day 13 - Calling the Disciples By Name

Read: Mark 3:7-19

Reflection:

I must have heard the names of the disciples, listed off like the books of the Bible and the tribes of Israel, a zillion times when I was a kid. The names were familiar, but did I ever think about the actual people who were called by those names? Nope. Not at all.

It's so easy to depersonalize others and see them as their title, position, or role: DTS leader, pastor, boss, teacher, barista, homeless person, or immigrant. It's easy to put a label on someone—with all the attached expectations, prejudices, or preconceived ideas—and then never give them any more of your attention.

Reading through the Bible, it's clear that God notices details. The names of people, tribes, cities, and landmarks fill page after page. The Bible isn't about generic people but about men and women with families, emotions, questions, and personalities. The details of these stories make them come alive and remind me there's no facet of my life unnoticed by God.

When Jesus chose the twelve disciples, the first thing listed in their job description was "that they would be with Him." These guys weren't faceless extras to Jesus—they were His friends. He knew them by name. He wanted to hang out with them. In the years to come, these disciples would learn many things and work hard to extend the kingdom, but their work and performance wasn't at the top of the list of importance.

There are days I feel quite confused about what it is I'm called to as a disciple. I stay busy, trying to make the most of my time. I go to meetings and write emails. I send letters and run errands. When I have a lot to do, it's easy to feel important. But I wonder… who would actually notice if I weren't around? Does Jesus notice me for who I am, or is He mostly interested in what I do for Him?

This passage brings me hope and sheds a different light on following Jesus. Jesus chose twelve specific men to be His disciples because He wanted to be *with* them. That says a lot about the value He puts on friendship and relationship. It says a lot about how He sees me, too. Jesus has called me to follow Him because He wants us to be together. He knows me by name. He knows the details of my life—the town where grew up, the family I came from, the things I dream of for the future. Who I am is significant to Him, and I am worthy of His time and attention.

Something to Think About:

1. Can you think of times in your life when you have felt replaceable?
2. Who are some of the people in your life who value you for *you*, not only for what you accomplish? How does it feel to be loved so unconditionally?
3. How does knowing that you are loved and chosen *to be with Jesus* affect the way you see yourself?

Action Steps:

1. Find a way to let a friend or family member know they are valuable to you for more than what they do.
2. As you interact with the people in your life today, how can you communicate they are valuable for more than what they do? What does this look like at the coffee shop? Grocery store? At work?
3. Look through your DTS journal (or blog, personal journal, etc.) and re-read the encouragements and affirmations from your classmates and staff, and the Scriptures/words God spoke to you. Let these soak in and touch your heart.

Going Deeper:

1. Take some time to think about this concept from the other side. Do you see Jesus for who He is, or only for what He can do for you? What's the

difference between the two? Take some time to think about and express how much you value Him for Him.

2. Spend some time with Jesus asking Him, "Jesus, how do you feel about me?" Listen as He speaks His truth over you. Write down what you think He may be saying and meditate on it. Share what you heard with someone you trust, asking them to confirm what you sensed from God.

Day 14 - Sunday Reflection

This week we've read about how Jesus is both willing and able to help those who come to Him in need. We've read about the beauty of friendship and the power of invitation. We've considered the temptation to judge and criticize others—especially when we feel insecure—and have been inspired by the way Jesus did what was good, no matter what the people around Him were doing.

Finally, we thought about the value God places on us, calling us by name, inviting us to follow Him and be *with* Him. It can be tempting to draw value from what we accomplish or how busy we are. Be careful not to let what you are doing or what you are trying to figure out consume all of your time, leaving nothing for God or the people around you.

Sabbath Review: Week Two

1. Connection. In the past week, who have you connected with? Think about family members, roommates, friends from DTS, people at church, work or school friends. How did you feel about the quality of the time you spent together? How well did you listen? Is there anything that could have made the time together better?

For the coming week, look for an opportunity to reach out to someone you don't know well. This could mean sitting with a stranger at church or in the lunch room, chatting with someone you don't know well at a party, or talking with a person who crosses your path in a different setting.

2. Service and Generosity. In what ways have you expressed a heart of service and generosity this week? Being willing to serve is a great way to express gratitude and love to others. Service and generosity can look like washing the dishes, taking out the garbage, giving someone a ride somewhere, or asking someone about their day and listening with your full attention. Service and generosity can look like colouring with a child, calling your grandma to say "hello," letting someone ahead of you in the grocery line, or letting someone else decide which movie to watch.

For the coming week, ask your pastor if there's anyone in your church or neighbourhood who could benefit from a few hours of your time. See if you could serve someone in need by mowing their lawn, running errands, or cooking a meal.

3. Self-care. How have you been taking care of yourself this week? Have you been getting enough sleep? Are you eating well? Are you drinking enough water? What are you doing for exercise? Have you made time for "play," for things you find truly enjoyable: things so fun for you that you lose track of time when doing them? (This could be reading, sports, crafting, hanging out with friends, you name it.)

For the coming week, pay attention to how much sleep you are getting. Are you still dealing with jetlag or trying to adjust to your current schedule? Having enough sleep can make a big difference in helping you cope with the stresses related to re-entry after DTS. If you aren't familiar with basic healthy sleep habits, get started learning about them here: www.sleepeducation.org/essentials-in-sleep/healthy-sleep-habits.

4. Spiritual Life. In what ways have you been able to connect with God this week? Where have you sensed His presence as you go about your daily life? Which habits (such as reading Scripture, worship, prayer, Bible study, etc.) have you been able to engage in? What do you sense God is saying to you these days? In what ways do you sense His encouragement and affirmation of you as His child?

For the coming week, make an appointment to spend time with God. Go somewhere special—to the park, on a hike, to a coffee shop or the beach. Instead of focusing on all the decisions you have to make, try to enjoy being in His presence.

Week Three

Day 15 - When Theory Becomes Reality

Read: Mark 3:20-30

Reflection:

ONE OF THE most important experiences of my DTS was that of being part of a healthy, loving team. In my team, I was no longer by myself all the time. I was accepted, and I belonged. We were in it together, both for good and for bad. I discovered that being part of a team requires give and take, and sometimes it's even extravagant giving and extravagant receiving as well!

There were definitely challenges, too. People on the team were very different from me, and I wasn't used to so much variety! Sure, I'd been friends with people from other places before, but the combination of different generations, nationalities, cultures, languages, denominations, and marital statuses was a lot to deal with at once!

However, what seemed odd about my teammates in the beginning became normal and beautiful as time went by. Learning to live and work with people different from me was an incredible gift. How rich we are in YWAM to have friends from around the world and from every walk of life. There are many benefits to seeing through other people's eyes and discovering more ways of thinking, speaking, and relating.

When people are different, it's easy—even natural—to be suspicious or get offended. In this passage, the scribes couldn't understand what Jesus was doing, and their response was to attack Him.

Jesus saw their attack as an opportunity to explain an important lesson to His disciples. A kingdom divided against itself cannot stand. There is strength in unity. At that point in His ministry, people didn't understand what Jesus was doing or why He had the authority to do miracles. However, it was clear He was doing good. How could Jesus be working for evil by doing what is right?

Through your DTS, you have been given a unique perspective on unity in diversity. You grew to love people you never would have chosen as friends. You overcame obstacles of language, culture, and nationality to build the body of Christ and share the gospel. You have something very important to say about how to express unity in the body of Christ. What may have once just been a theory to you has now become reality.

Next time you see something in the Church you don't understand or that is just plain irritating, remember what you experienced in DTS. There is room for a lot of beautiful variety in the family of God. What's more, you are called to be a peace-maker and a unifier. Look for ways to build bridges and make connections with believers who are different from you.

Something to Think About:

1. Who did you meet at DTS (roommates, teachers, staff, classmates) that had very different views or opinions from you? What did you learn from these people?
2. Who in your life right now is very different from you? How can you appreciate these differences and see them as strengths?

Action Steps:

1. How much do you know about the body of Christ in the place where you are living? Do some research and consider visiting a gathering or worship service in a culture or language different from your own. Did you go to Vietnam on outreach? See if there's a Vietnamese fellowship in your city. Is there an international students' lunch at your university? Think about different ways to welcome foreigners to your country.
2. Do something to serve those who you are living with today: empty the garbage, wash the dishes, clean the bathroom. Let Jesus' servant-love flow out of you today.

Going Deeper:

1. Read Ephesians 4:1-6. What insights does this passage shed on our source of unity in the body of Christ? What attitudes are we to develop in regard to those who are different from us? How did your DTS experience help you to appreciate what you have in common with believers who are different from you?
2. One of YWAM's Foundational Values addresses the idea of unity in diversity. How was this value displayed in your DTS, and how can you continue to embrace it, even if you are no longer in YWAM?

> *Value 8: Be international and interdenominational*
>
> *YWAM is international and interdenominational in its global scope as well as its local constituency. We believe that ethnic, linguistic, and denominational diversity, along with redeemed aspects of culture, are positive factors that contribute to the health and growth of the mission.*

Day 16 - Are We Related?

Read: Mark 3:31-35

Reflection:

Jesus wasn't suffering from amnesia when He asked, "Who are my mother and my brothers?" Instead, He was using this conversation about relatives and family to point out that our faith is to expand and instruct our definition of family.

Families come in many shapes and sizes, and each one has strengths and weaknesses. Even the most idyllic family cannot express everything family is supposed to be. We can always learn more from others about the care, kindness, and respect that builds strong relationships. I hope DTS was a place you were able to deepen your understanding of what loving relationships look like.

I grew up in a small family—just my dad, brother, and me. You can imagine how the community life of DTS, with roommates, game nights, and continual activity was a big change for me. I liked it, but it took some getting used to.

Day after day during DTS, and then on outreach, I discovered my heart was expanding in its capacity to care about others. People who were strangers at the beginning of DTS became near and dear. With God as my Father, all His children are part of my family too. The line between "us" and "them," or between "my family" and "everyone else," began to fade. I realized I was much less alone in the world than I thought.

In addition to this, as I experienced the love and acceptance of brothers and sisters in Christ, I was learning about how to love my biological family better. I was becoming kinder, more patient, more grateful, less selfish.

Jesus' words are an encouragement to grow in love. Love

isn't something reserved for a small group of those closest to us. We are to love extravagantly, and with God's help, a year from now, we will be able to love more and better than we do today.

Something to Think About:

1. What do you think Jesus was getting at when He asked, "Who are my mother and brothers?"
2. How has learning about God as your Father impacted your ability to love and care for others, even those who are different from you?
3. Who are the people in your life right now toward whom you are finding it most difficult to be loving?

Action Steps:

1. How has your experience in DTS altered your ability to love your family members? How can you express love to someone in your family today?
2. At times it seems easier to be polite and considerate to a stranger or guest than a family member or close friend. Reflect on the people you've spent time with since your return from DTS. Have you been considerate and appreciative in these relationships, or have you been taking people for granted? Is there anything you'd like to adjust in your relationships?

Going Deeper:

1. Pray the Lord's Prayer a few times throughout the day today (for example, at meals, while waiting for meetings to begin, when you brush your teeth, etc.). Picture God as Father to all His children. As you pray, imagine some of the individuals and groups who are in the family of God. How does thinking about these people change the way you pray or feel?

Day 17 - Lessons From a Relaxed Gardener

Read: Mark 4:1-20

Reflection:

I've planted a few gardens in my life. First as a kid helping my dad, then on outreach in the Pacific, then in various pots and planters in big city apartments. It takes a lot of work to get the ground ready for planting. There are always weeds, rocks, hard patches, and areas that are too wet or too dry. I've lost count of the blisters, splinters, and sunburns I've earned before even a single seed reached the earth.

Once the seeds have been planted, there is a lot of waiting to endure. While you wait, you also wonder: Were the seeds any good? Is the soil too dry? Is there enough sun?

Too much sun? Are insects devouring my seeds at this very moment?

Like the scenarios Jesus describes, many things can prevent a seed from growing. A lot can stop a seed from becoming a plant that bears fruit. Gardening is stressful! And when I realize Jesus isn't talking only about seeds and plants, but friends, family, and colleagues… I feel even worse.

The work of the kingdom is not for wimps. Sharing Christ, asking for miracles, and interceding for the transformation of hearts requires much hard work. You know this already. You have experienced it in DTS, on outreach, and where you are right now. Working in God's field may involve blisters and splinters. Caring about people and having their best interest in mind will make your life less comfortable. It will require time, and it may even demand sacrifices.

And then, after you've done all you can, served and loved and given of yourself, you might not see the results you've hoped for. The seeds you've watered and sheltered may get stolen or trampled on.

What's equally frustrating is that we don't get to decide which seeds will bear fruit and which ones will go to waste. What we can do is be faithful, generous, and considerate to all people. We can be attentive to the leading of Holy Spirit around us. He is at work, and we are invited to work *with* Him.

There's nothing in the story to give the impression the Sower is freaked out about all that might ruin the seeds He is casting around. Shouldn't He be more worried? More anxious? Stingier with His seeds? Surely God is *more* concerned with His field and His harvest than I am!

Then I remembered something I'd learned as a gardener:

there are lots of ways and lots of times to plant seeds. If the ground isn't ready this spring, then there's work to be done for next year. If one field gets too much sun, then a better location can be found. If a plant can't handle the elements, it can be started in a greenhouse.

God is at work around us in more ways that we can see or guess. Don't be afraid to work hard and get your hands dirty in His field; but don't carry the weight of needing to make something happen. Sow all the seeds you can. And while you're at it, pay attention to the soil of your own life as well. Don't let your desire to change the world choke out the growth God has for you in this season.

Something to Think About:

1. As you think about your personal journey of faith, which parts of the parable can you relate to? Were you hard ground, rocky soil, choked by weeds, or good soil? Can you see times and ways the condition of your soil has changed?
2. Have you ever had the opportunity to garden or take care of plants? What were some things you had to remember and pay attention to? Did the plants flourish or wilt under your care? What character traits of God come to mind when you think about Him as a gardener?

Action Steps:

1. Spend some time drawing or painting this parable as an act of intercession. What is going on around

you right now? Who are the people who have heard the word? Who is represented by the rocky ground? Where might birds be trying to steal away seeds that have been planted?

2. Read verses 13-20 again, and ask Holy Spirit to bring to your attention anything in your life He'd like to show you. How are your roots? How deeply are you planted? Are there worries or concerns trying to choke your growth?

Going Deeper:

1. Check out the website iamsecond.com for inspiring videos and blogs about people who have discovered Christ. Many of the films tell of the difficult journey of pain and brokenness and remind us that God is at work all around us. One film that touches me a great deal is the testimony of Brian Welch, lead guitarist for the band Korn.
2. Choose something living you could plant and go for it! You could pick something as simple as sprouting a bean, to planting a row of carrots, to starting a box garden on your balcony. Pay attention to what you can learn about growth, patience, and perseverance through this process.

Day 18 - Put That Lamp On A Table!

Read: Mark 4:21-25

Reflection:

Have you ever heard of someone buying a spiffy new piece of technology for themselves, then coming home and shoving it under some junk in the attic or putting it in the garage with the recycling? I never have.

When you're given something of great value, there is always the possibility it will get ruined. But to truly appreciate what you have been given, you must accept that risks are part of life, and then open the box and learn how to use what you have to its utmost capability. A new tablet or phone just cries out to be used.

In the same way, Jesus says the good news is for sharing with others. You put a lamp on the table to brighten a whole room. Something so good and so easy to share with others would be wasted under a table or hidden in a cupboard.

The light of a lamp, like the beauty of the gospel, can be shared with many people and not lose any of its power. In fact, the more people who are drawn to the light, the more beauty we see reflected in it.

You have been given so much in your DTS: truth, friendships, encouragement, experiences with Jesus, and the list goes on. You have seen His love at work in your own life and reflected in the lives of others. It's one thing to brag about all you've been able to do and see, using your experiences to put yourself above others; but it's a totally different thing to tell stories that point people to God and stir up curiosity to discover more about Him.

Don't hide what God's done in you or let the fear of "doing it wrong" keep you from giving some of these treasures away to others. Words of encouragement, reminders of God's love, kindness, and small acts of service don't cost much, but they have great potential to shine some light.

Something to Think About:

1. Would you say you have a tendency to be more planned and cautious in life, or to be more impulsive and spontaneous? How can your unique approach to life be a strength when it comes to partnering with God to share His light with others?
2. What are some fears or concerns that hold you back from sharing God's light with others?
3. Would you say you are someone who prefers to give, or to receive? How do you feel about that?

Action Steps:

1. What are three truths that impacted you significantly during DTS? Is there some way you could share those truths with others? What would it look like?
2. If you haven't done so already, consider writing a blog post, FB post, making a YouTube video, or finding some other way to report back on what you experienced during DTS. The goal of what you create is not to get the most likes or hits, but to express something of who God is and what He

has done in your life. There are so many out there who need to hear or need to be reminded of His love and goodness.

Going Deeper:

1. Being able to shine in the world involves knowing who you are, how you've been created, and what you can uniquely bring to each situation you are in. One great resource to help you discover more about the unique way God created you is a test called *StrengthsFinder*. For more info about this online test which will identify five of your top strengths, buy *StrengthsFinder 2.0* by Tom Rath or visit www.strengthsfinder.com.
2. Take some time to think about the activities, hobbies, or interests you had as a child, teen, or young adult. What opportunities are there for you to "revisit" some of these to see if you still enjoy them? How might these interests be connected to talents or gifts that God has given to you?

Day 19 - He Himself Does Not Know

Read: Mark 4:26-34

Reflection:

What strikes me as I read these parables is the contrast between what the farmer does and what God does. Jesus tells many stories about plants and farming in Mark. If you grew up near a farm, these stories make more sense than if you grew up in the city. But no matter where you're from, stories about living things remind us there are aspects of life and growth beyond our control.

Wherever you involve something living in a situation, it becomes more complicated. If you've been to a live nativity or tried to bake something with the help of small children, you know what I'm talking about! No matter how diligent and hardworking a farmer may be, she knows there are *many* things she cannot control. Wind, sun, birds, mold, insects, hail…you get the idea. A farmer cannot control everything. She cannot guarantee results. And neither can you. I think this is what Jesus is trying to get at in these stories.

But instead of encouraging us to work harder, always be on time, control what we can, and never slack off (which is the direction I'd go), Jesus has a different angle on how to live in a world that we can't control. He explains how this farmer completes his work and then goes to bed. That's it. As the days go by, the seeds sprout, grow, and develop. The farmer doesn't know how it happens. But when the time is right, the farmer harvests the crop. End of story. No claims of having it all figured out.

DTS was a focused time of sowing seeds. Day after day you shared Christ with strangers, children, at churches, on the streets. You prayed for people at restaurants, on the metro, while you were buying train tickets. Even on days off, you took opportunities to talk about Christ.

That season of intensity doesn't last forever. This is one of the most challenging transitions for DTS grads to make. Many feel guilty if they aren't approaching a stranger every 3.4 minutes to talk about God. Others are bored by the slow pace of life.

This parable tells us it's important to remember: God has a part, and we have a part. Us YWAMers love to say, "Just hear God's voice and obey it"; yet there are days when what we are supposed to be doing is not so clear. What encourages me, though, is the reminder that God *is* at work, even when I can't see it. Growth in people's lives does not depend on me. I don't have to understand how it works. My role is to be faithful in what God has shown me to do. Then, like the farmer, I can relax and rejoice in what happens around me.

If you have experienced guilt or boredom since DTS ended, let me turn your attention back to the farmer. He planted his seeds, went to bed, slept, and got up the next day. He lived with peace, confident he'd done his part. He wasn't trying to plant seeds in another farmer's field or squeeze more rows between what was already there. He trusted the One who was able to make the plants grow. It's possible he felt bored or impatient during the growing season. That's totally normal. But he reminded himself he was part of something bigger than himself, and he watched as new life sprang up from places that seemed ordinary and lifeless.

Something to Think About:

1. How can you tell if you are in a season of planting seeds or watching them grow? Which season do you think you are in at the moment?
2. What was the attitude/posture of the farmer in the parable? What attitude will you choose to have during this current season of life?
3. What's your understanding of your part and God's part in the work of the kingdom? Is there anything God would like to highlight to you about the partnership between you and Him?
4. Look back on your experience in DTS. What are some ways you planted kingdom seeds in the lives of those you met and served?

Action Steps:

1. Make a list of the activities or projects that you are involved in right now. These can be formal (teaching Sunday school) or informal (praying for coworkers, practicing gratitude). Prayerfully ask God to help you see what your part is in each activity and what He's responsible for.
2. What was your favourite activity during outreach? Research if there are similar volunteering opportunities where you are now, and treat this place as your mission field for however long you stay.
3. Do you know any farmers or gardeners? Ask them if you could join them at work one day or get a tour of their field. Talk with them about what's

involved in planting, growing, and caring for living plants. What is their perspective on what they are in control of and what things are out of their control?

Going Deeper:

1. How much do you know about mustard seeds and plants? Take some time to learn about them. Consider what Jesus was trying to communicate through this parable.
2. Check out the video "The Mustard Seed" on the movingworks.org website.
3. Meditate on this quote from the Christian author George MacDonald: "He that believes shall not make haste…There is plenty of time. You must not imagine that the result depends on you, or me. The question is, are you having a hand in the work God is doing? It shows no faith in God to make frantic efforts or lamentations. God will do his work in his time in his way. Our responsibility is merely to stand ready and available and to go where he sends and do what comes our way."

Day 20 - An Invitation to Know Him Better

Read: Mark 4:35-41

Reflection:

My favorite books growing up were adventures. I'd get lost in the pages, picturing myself as the hero, on the horse with a sword or jumping over tall buildings, saving the day when no one else could. Normal life seemed, well, too *normal.* Give me more excitement, more danger, more odds to overcome! Glory was waiting around the corner!

In Mark 4, Jesus' disciples were still learning the ropes of following Jesus. They had seen a number of miracles already, but some of the things Jesus did still surprised them. Taking a nap during a life-threatening storm, for example. Ordering the wind and waves to obey was another one.

Maybe you can relate to the feeling you're still learning the ropes when it comes to following Christ. Maybe you wonder what you've gotten yourself into. You are confident you've seen Him at work. You have experienced His power firsthand. But there are situations where you find yourself scratching your head in confusion. "Is He even awake?" and "Does He realize what's going on?" you may ask. "What crazy thing will He do next?" and "What does He expect from me?" you may wonder at other times.

Jesus' response to His disciples freaking out in the boat was an invitation to know Him better. It was as if He was saying, "There's still more to me than what you've discovered thus far. Don't be afraid. Trust me, and let me show you who I am."

As amazing as my DTS was, there were also times that were scary, intense, and painful. As tempting as it was to run away from the difficult parts of the DTS, I'm so glad I stuck with it. In the midst of the tears or sleepless nights, I learned how to look to Jesus when I was afraid and confused. I learned how to ask for help from my teammates and staff. I discovered I don't have to figure everything out on my own. And that conclusion was worth every tear and frustration.

Today might be a wonderful day for you. It might be sunny, hopeful, and relaxing where you are. If so, I'm glad to hear it. On the other hand, today may be a day of clouds and wind, darkness and loneliness.

Regardless of the circumstances of the moment, let me remind you that Jesus is present with you. He will never abandon you. Sunshine or storm, He cares about what happens to you. He's aware of what's going on, and His response to your fear and your joy is an invitation to know Him more. Will you take Him up on His offer?

Something to Think About:

1. What are some of the ways you experienced Jesus' power during your DTS?
2. How have you seen Him at work in and around you since you finished DTS?
3. What are the areas in your life where you are worried or afraid at the moment?

Action Steps:

1. Make a list of five events/experiences from DTS that showed God's power. Pray for someone involved in one of those stories. Pray for God to remind that person of His love today.

2. Search the internet or your own files for a photo that signifies peace and God's presence to you.
3. Jesus is inviting you to know Him more. Take some time to journal about that invitation and your response to it.

Going Deeper:

1. Read Psalm 42. Of the emotions the writer expresses, which can you relate to the most?
2. Write out Psalm 42:11 and put it somewhere you can see it.

Day 21 - Sunday Reflection

This week we were reminded of the value of unity and our ability to grow in love over time—even towards those who are difficult to love. We learned from the gardener that working in God's field is hard work, but it is also work that can be filled with peace as we trust the results to God. We don't have to fix everything, change everyone, or answer every question in the world. Learning how to adjust to the new pace of life after DTS can be difficult, but God is with us, just as He was in DTS, and He can show us the way forward.

Sabbath Review: Week Three

1. Connection. In the past week, who have you connected with? Think about family members, roommates, friends from DTS, people at church, work or school friends. How did you feel about the quality of the time you spent together? How well did you listen? Is there anything that could have made the time together better?

For the coming week, print a photo and deliver or mail it to someone who will be surprised by your thoughtfulness.

2. Service and Generosity. In what ways have you expressed a heart of service and generosity this week? Being willing to serve is a great way to express gratitude and love to others. Service and generosity can look like washing the dishes, taking out the garbage, giving someone a ride somewhere, or asking someone about their day and listening with your full attention. Service and generosity can look like colouring with a child, calling your grandma to say "hello," letting someone ahead of you in the grocery line, or letting someone else decide which movie to watch.

For the coming week, what would it look like for you to give "a gift of words" to people around you? Something as simple as "hello," "I appreciate your service," or "I'm glad we got the chance to talk" can go a long way.

3. Self-care. How have you been taking care of yourself this week? Have you been getting enough sleep? Are you eating well? Are you drinking enough water? What are you doing for exercise? Have you made time for "play," for things you find truly enjoyable: things so fun for you that you lose track of time when doing them? (This could be reading, sports, crafting, hanging out with friends, you name it.)

For the coming week, make sure you are getting enough of both *alone* time and *people* time. Based on your personality, the amount of time you need in each of these categories will be different from others around you. Don't be afraid to take more time to be alone if you need it, or to look for ways to be with people if you need that.

4. Spiritual Life. In what ways have you been able to connect with God this week? Where have you sensed His presence as you go about your daily life? Which habits (such as reading Scripture, worship, prayer, Bible study, etc.) have you been able to engage in? What do you sense God is saying to you these days? In what ways do you sense His encouragement and affirmation of you as His child?

For the coming week, ask around for recommendations of a good book, blog, or podcast that can strengthen your relationship with God.

Week Four

Day 22 - Your Story is Worth Telling

Read: Mark 5:1-20

Reflection:

THERE ARE a great deal of things I don't know about pigs or about demon-possessed people. Maybe you feel the same way, and that's cool. What grabs my heart in this story is the description of the man with demons. Mark writes, "No one was able to bind him anymore," and "No one was strong enough to tame him." The situation with this man was so out of control, the entire city had given up on him. No one had any idea what to do. So everyone did the best they could to ignore him.

That is, until Jesus came to town.

We've read enough about Jesus to suspect He will say

something or do something, and He most certainly does. Is it surprising that God uses what is most hopeless and difficult in this man's life to demonstrate His power and concern for him? Perhaps you have seen God do something similar in your life—meet you in a place of brokenness and powerlessness to finally get through to you with His love.

As a child and teen, I was extremely shy. I constantly worried what people thought of me. I was anxious about my appearance and concerned with how I came across. I wanted to make sure I was always right and did everything right. I imagined every person in the hallway and every passerby was noticing all my flaws and mistakes. I was afraid of a lot of things. I was sure my entire town thought me a lost cause.

I went to DTS straight out of high school. I was seventeen years old and a walking hurricane of insecurity, defensiveness, and determination. A lot changed for me during DTS. As months immersed in community and the love of God went by, I became calmer, less fearful, and more confident.

I'm so thankful Jesus "came to my town" and did for me what no one else had been able to do. I'm not surprised the demon-possessed man wanted to follow Jesus. I would have too, if I'd been in his place. But Jesus wouldn't let him. Instead, Jesus directed the man to return home and tell the story of what the Master had done: how He had mercy on him.

Like this man, you and I have been "sent" by Jesus to share the story of what He has done in our lives. Your story is incredible, and it's worth telling. Let's follow the example of the man from Gerasenes and share our story with others.

Something to Think About:

1. What are some things God has done for you that you could share with your family or friends? How could you express these things in ways your family and friends could understand?
2. How would you say you are different now than you were when you left for DTS? Some changes take time to work themselves out, so don't be discouraged if you don't see quick or dramatic changes.
3. In the devotional, I wrote that God often meets us in areas of weakness and pain in order to get through to us with His love. Has this been the case in your life? What are some examples of times God has met you in your pain?

Action Steps:

1. If you keep a journal or blog, or if you wrote a letter to God at the beginning of DTS, go back and read what you wrote a few months ago. How does it compare to how you think and feel now?
2. Make a timeline of your life, listing significant events, relationships, and experiences. Go back over the timeline and add ways you can see God has been at work. What do you notice about the story of your life so far?

Going Deeper:

1. Respond in some creative manner to the phrase, "What great things the Lord has done for you, and how He has had mercy on you." You could draw, paint, write, dance, collage, cook, blog, sing, run—you name it!
2. Just as we read about the man living among the tombs, the world is full of people and situations that don't have a "quick fix" (or may not have any "fix" at all). What are the situations in your life, neighbourhood, city, or nation that no one knows how to address? How do you feel when you think about these situations? Instead of quickly trying to change the situation or fix the people who came to your mind, try to sit with God in the pain. Ask Him to show how His heart breaks for these people. Let Him meet you in this place of sadness and pain.

Day 23 - Why Did He Have It So Easy - Or Did He?

Read: Mark 5:21-34

Reflection:

In the world of commercials, you snap your fingers and see instant change. On cooking shows, you fast-forward through hours in the oven, and huge turkeys and cakes are done in a few minutes. On the sports channel, you see highlights and winners but skip over the practices and boring drills.

Why isn't life more like TV?

When you read today's passage, it's easy to think Jesus simply snapped His fingers (twice if necessary) and miracles came out of thin air. Why did He have it so easy?

However, if you look through the gospels, you will see Jesus doing a lot of training and practicing behind the scenes. He often slipped away to spend time with the Father. He read and studied the Scriptures a ton. He spent years learning to tune into the voice of the Spirit so He could do these amazing miracles when they were needed.

Maybe you're new to life with God—new to hearing His voice and responding. Maybe you're new to letting the Spirit work through you to touch the world.

If so, don't be discouraged by the challenges you experience. You are learning. You are growing. You are doing an awesome job! Think of how far you've come since you showed up at your DTS half a year ago.

God promises that His Spirit will teach and guide us. Jesus is our example, and He is a patient teacher. This journey of knowing and working with Him has just started, and trust me, there is much more to come!

Something to Think About:

1. Think through the activities you did on your DTS outreach. Which of them were new to you? Which things got easier the more you practiced?

2. Are you dealing with something now that is difficult and doesn't seem to be getting any better?
3. Which types of spiritual activities (worship, reading Scripture, prayer, fellowship, etc.) brought you life and inspiration during DTS?

Action Steps:

1. Send an encouraging note or Scripture verse to a DTS classmate or friend.
2. Use a Bible program and do a word search on "encourage" and "encouragement." What can you learn about this topic, and what does God say about encouraging us?
3. Pray for someone you know who's sick and needs to experience God's healing power.
4. Think about a creative way to work some of those things you enjoyed most about DTS into your life this week: organize a one-on-one conversation over Skype, find a Bible-reading plan online, or have a worship session in your bedroom.

Going Deeper:

1. Have a conversation with an older Christian you admire, either in person, by phone, or online. Ask them to talk about how God has helped them through difficult times, and be listening for what you can learn from them. Thank them for their time and let them know one specific way in which what they have told you has been helpful.
2. Look back over your own life. What part of the

process of becoming more like Jesus happened quickly for you? Which parts of the process have taken a longer time? What is one area you would like to invite God to be at work in you now?

Day 24 - Making Time for a Twelve-Year Old

Read: Mark 5:35-43

Reflection:

What was your life like when you were twelve years old? When I was twelve, my parents had recently divorced, and I spent a lot of time alone. Few people had time for me or gave me a lot of attention. I generally stayed quiet and tried to stay in the background. Attention usually meant I was about to be asked for something or be put on the spot, and I hated that.

It's remarkable to me that Jesus gave so much time and attention to the twelve-year-old girl in this passage. She hadn't done anything impressive or shocking to catch His notice. She wasn't doing *anything*, as a matter of fact, because she was dead.

In a world that pays special attention to the wealthy, to famous celebrities, and to those in positions of power, there are huge numbers of people who go largely unnoticed. Who has time to care about every kid, every sick person, every old lady or panhandler? And even if you were to pay attention to some of these people, what good would it do?

Jesus, however, was willing to make time for a sick child and for the request of this girl's father. Yes, her father was an important figure in the synagogue, but she was just a child and not very significant in the grand scheme of things. But Jesus' commitment to her and His willingness to go out of His way to help her speaks loudly about how important she was in His eyes. When He arrived at the home and was told the girl had died, He didn't see this as a way to get off the hook. Instead, He summoned His friends around Him, went to see the girl, and partnered with God to bring her back to life.

Jesus' response to those in need says a lot about what He's like and gives insight about how we are to live as His followers. If Jesus was okay with being interrupted during His work, how much more should I be okay when I'm interrupted? If Jesus had time for a dead twelve-year-old, who might He want me to make space for in my life?

Something to Think About:

1. What is easier for you to give: your time, your money, or your attention?
2. How do you respond when you are interrupted? What does this say about how you view your time and your agenda?
3. Can you think of someone who noticed you when you were a kid? How did the attention make you feel? What did the person do to make you feel special?

Action Steps:

1. Send a note or thank you to someone in your life who makes time for you. Let them know how good it feels to be important to them.
2. Who are the people in your daily life who get passed by or ignored? Think of a way to give the gift of your time this week (sharing a coffee, offering to drive them somewhere, volunteering to babysit, etc.).
3. Do you know any twelve-year-olds? Think about what you could do for/with them that would affirm their value and worth.

Going Deeper:

1. Plan a special outing with a child or youth you know (ice cream trip, movie, or amusement park, etc.). If you don't know any kids that well, pray for an opportunity to invest in a young person.
2. Ask God to show you which kids/youth in your community (family, church, neighbourhood) you could give some time to. Write their birth date on your calendar and remember to send them a birthday card. Congratulate these kids when they complete a grade in school, or attend one of their sporting or musical events. It might seem small to you, but making time for children can make a big difference to them.

Day 25 - Home Sweet Home

Read: Mark 6:1-6

Reflection:

When you are in a strange city or foreign country, the thought of *home* often stirs up nostalgia and warm, fuzzy feelings. Home is the place of total comfort, good night sleeps, welcome, and acceptance. Everything tastes and feels better when you're at home. That is, at least, until you're back. That's when you quickly realize that the annoyances and frustrations you were glad to leave behind are still there.

Nevertheless, home is a place where you're known. Your history, family, successes, and failures are common knowledge. There is comfort and beauty in being known by others, but there are challenges too. People have ideas about how you will act, how you will speak, and what's important to you. Home can be like water in a powerful river, pulling you in a direction, whether you want to go there or not.

When Jesus visited His hometown, His presence and message were met with mixed results. Some people were amazed by what He had to say. Others were skeptical, thinking they knew everything about Him.

It's hard to predict how people will respond to your DTS experience. Some will be excited for you. Some will be critical. Some will act like you never even left. These responses can be painful, encouraging, confusing.

Jesus didn't demand people at home adjust the way they saw Him by pushing and pushing until they figured out who He was. He did what He could, shared what He had, and then continued on His way.

It's not your job to make sure everyone at home gets excited about God or interested in missions. You can relax, trusting that just as God led you, He can lead those around you.

Instead of getting flustered or frustrated if people respond differently to your homecoming than you expected, try to view this season as an opportunity for your changed life to preach a message that will point people to Jesus.

Something to Think About:

1. What emotions do you think Jesus felt during this visit to His hometown?
2. What has been the response of friends and family to your experience in DTS and to your return?
3. Have you been surprised by any of these responses? If so, how have you reacted?

Action Steps:

1. Are there any people who expressed interest in hearing about your DTS who you haven't been able to connect with yet? Contact them to arrange a time to get together. Make sure you take the time to find out what they have been learning and doing while you were away.
2. Can you relate to the tendency to label or judge

people based on their background or family, instead of taking the time to listen to what they are actually saying? Take a few minutes to reflect on the interactions you've had with people in the past days and weeks. See if there's anything the Holy Spirit would bring to mind.

Going Deeper:

1. Leaving home for a season and coming back again can give you a new perspective on the familiar. Take a morning or afternoon and spend it in your neighbourhood. Pay attention to the people, buildings, parks, schools, businesses, nature, streets, and so on. Ask God to show you His heart for your hometown. Try to see the beauty and distinctness of this place with eyes of gratitude and hope. If you feel led, consider expressing your gratitude for something you appreciate about your hometown. For example, you could write a note to the mayor, take cookies to the fire station, volunteer at a neighbourhood clean-up, or compliment a neighbour on the beauty of their flower garden.

Day 26 - You Are The Equipment

Read: Mark 6:7-13

Reflection:

I've traveled a lot during my years in YWAM, but I still haven't got the packing thing down to an art. Usually I bring more stuff than I need and manage to forget some important items at the same time. How does that happen?

Jesus is sending His disciples on a big mission without Him. They are nervous, wondering what to bring, what's going to happen, how they will manage without Him by their side. His encouraging advice is this: "Don't think you need a lot of extra equipment for this. You are the equipment" (v.8, *The Message*). Wow! Everything they are going to need they already have. Could that be true? What about spare batteries? Toothpaste? Bible app? Portable speakers?

This is a verse I like to read to outreach teams before heading to the airport to remind them—Friends, you are the equipment. God's Spirit is in you, and you have a team around you. You've got this!

Most outreach teams take batteries with them, and toothpaste, and other supplies as well. Nothing wrong with that. What usually happens, however, is the most fruitful ministry and deepest relationships are the result of each team member simply being him or herself and responding to the leading of the Spirit in the normal things of life. Am I right?

Now you are back home again. No team. No special equipment. No one-on-one. No small group. Maybe even no roommate anymore. What to do?

Two things stand out to me.

1. Attempting to give away as much from your DTS experience as you can will keep you busy for a long time! What I mean is: the truth, love, and friendship you were given have changed you, so what if you tried to share those same things with other people? They say teaching what you have learned to someone else is the best way to really learn it.

2. It's not bad to need things. When you ask for help moving apartments, need to borrow a ladder, or catch a ride to church with someone, you are building friendship and community. Being in need is a great way to make new friends, and once someone has helped you, they are a lot more likely to ask for your help in return.

Something to Think About:

1. What do you think about Jesus' statement, "You are the equipment"?
2. What are some of the "tools" you gained during DTS that are part of you now (learning to study the Bible, praying for others, courage to talk to strangers, etc.)?
3. How have people responded to what you have shared about your DTS? Have some people been curious and interested? Have others been indifferent or hostile? How do you feel about these responses? What advice does Jesus give about dealing with different responses?

Action Steps:

1. Did you realize that in the six months of your DTS, you have received more Christian training than most Christians around the world will get in their lifetime? Meditate on that for a while.
2. Think about a piece of equipment you received during DTS, and come up with one way you can use it today.
3. What's something you can do today (either giving or receiving) that will build relationship and community with someone in your life? Do it.

Going Deeper:

1. *To whom much has been given, much is required* (Luke 12:48). Think about how rich you are! How would God want to use you to extend His kingdom today? Are there opportunities for service or giving that you can respond to? What would you like to accomplish with God in the next year of your life?
2. In DTS, there may have been many situations where you were uncomfortable. Often, God meets us in those places precisely because what is in front of us is too big for us to do on our own. Talk with God or write Him a letter as you consider what it means for you to follow Him "outside of your comfort zone."

Day 27 - A Response to Suffering and Pain

Read: Mark 6:14–29

Reflection:

No matter how many times I read this story, I'm never sure what to make of it. Not really the best material for a Sunday school classroom and colouring book pages. It's shocking and sobering, thought-provoking and horrifying.

So, what are we supposed to make of tragic stories and senseless violence we hear about or experience? Do we skip over these verses and move to something more edifying? Can we ignore the parts that make us angry, confused, and upset? Sometimes there's nothing you can do. Sometimes there is a way to respond.

Instead of quoting clichés about suffering and pain, I invite you to think about your response to the suffering and pain around you.

Are you an avoider? A confronter? Do you run away from pain and loss? Do you take steps toward it? Do you wish people would talk about their pain more, or less?

A few years ago I read Bill Hybel's book, *Just Walk Across the Room.* The premise to the book, as suggested in the title, is if we will take the small step to walk across the room to start a conversation with a stranger, or to ask someone if she needs help, or to say a simple hello, God will go with us and show us what to do next. If we simply do what we can —position ourselves to respond to God's leading—He will show us each step and help us be a witness for Him.

Something to Think About:

1. Would you say you are more of an avoider or a confronter? How helpful has this been for you in your life and relationships?
2. How do you generally respond to suffering, pain, tragedy, and loss? What are some examples of this from recent days?
3. How have others responded to you during difficult times in your life? Do you wish the response had been different in some way? If so, how?

Action Steps:

1. Who do you know who is suffering from loss or grief right now? Consider a practical something you could do to show you care. Even if you don't know what to do, think about the "just walk across the room" idea. Just pick up the phone. Just drive to their house. Just sit next to them at church. Ask Holy Spirit to lead you step by step in reaching out to this person.
2. Watch the short video "Bettie Goes to Jail" on the movingworks.org website. It's a six-minute video about Bettie's willingness to follow God's leading to reach out to those in need. In what ways are you challenged or inspired by this woman?

Going Deeper:

1. Read *Just Walk Across the Room*, by Bill Hybels.

2. Read one of these books about grief and loss:

- *A Severe Mercy* by Sheldon Vanauken
- *Where is God When it Hurts?* by Philip Yancey
- *The Problem of Pain* by C. S. Lewis

Day 28 - Sunday Reflection

This week we have been encouraged to tell the story of what God has done in our lives. We have been reminded that change and growth take time—so be patient with yourself. We've seen the way Jesus placed value on children, and how a visit to His hometown was rather rocky. We were encouraged by how much we received in DTS and asked what it would look like for us to give these things away to others.

But it's not all about what we can do for others; asking for help is a great way to build relationships. A healthy life includes both giving and receiving. Finally, we considered the realities of suffering and pain in the world and how difficult it can be to know how to respond to loss and grief.

Sabbath Review: Week Four

1. Connection. In the past week, who have you connected with? Think about family members, roommates, friends from DTS, people at church, work or school friends. How did you feel about the quality of the time you spent together? How well did you listen? Is there anything that could have made the time together better?

For the coming week, look for opportunities to connect with people who are younger than you.

2. Service and Generosity. In what ways have you expressed a heart of service and generosity this week? Being willing to serve is a great way to express gratitude and love to others. Service and generosity can look like washing the dishes, taking out the garbage, giving someone a ride somewhere, or asking someone about their day and listening with your full attention. Service and generosity can look like colouring with a child, calling your grandma to say "hello," letting someone ahead of you in the grocery line, or letting someone else decide which movie to watch.

For the coming week, think about something you could do to care for or beautify your neighbourhood, such as picking up garbage, sweeping the sidewalk, or planting flowers.

3. Self-care. How have you been taking care of yourself this week? Have you been getting enough sleep? Are you eating well? Are you drinking enough water? What are you doing for exercise? Have you made time for "play," for things you find truly enjoyable: things so fun for you that you lose track of time when doing them? (This could be reading, sports, crafting, hanging out with friends, you name it.)

For the coming week, consider how active you are being with your body. Are you getting enough exercise and movement on a regular basis? There are many apps out there to measure and motivate you toward being active.

4. Spiritual Life. In what ways have you been able to connect with God this week? Where have you sensed His presence as you go about your daily life? Which habits (such as reading Scripture, worship, prayer, Bible study, etc.) have you been able to engage in? What do you sense God is saying to you these days? In what ways do you sense His encouragement and affirmation of you as His child?

For the coming week, go on a walk or field trip with God. Think of a special place to visit in your hometown or nearby. Enjoy being with God on the journey there and back, as well as at the destination itself.

Week Five

Day 29 - He Felt Compassion For Them

Read: Mark 6:30-44

Reflection:

LIKE ME, you may wonder where emotions belong in the life of an adult. As a kid, it's pretty simple—however you feel comes out in tears, screams, or laughter. As adults, we are still learning when to let emotions lead us and when to ignore them as we make decisions.

Jesus is remarkably wise as a human. He allows Himself to experience the full range of emotions, and He knows how to use them to share truth and build relationship with others.

When Jesus sees the crowd, He is moved with compassion. His compassion leads to action—first He teaches about the kingdom, and then He feeds the crowd with bread and fish instead of sending them away hungry.

In a culture where some leaders consider themselves above the common people, Jesus is willing to be affected by those around Him. He didn't harden His heart to the hungry or become irritated by the crowd's endless needs.

To recap the events:

- Jesus sees the needs (a crowd of people, desperate and vulnerable, like sheep without a shepherd),
- He feels compassion,
- He responds by giving truth through teaching,
- He notices physical hunger,
- He discovers what's available (two fish, five loaves),
- He thanks the Father in advance and expects Him to do something amazing,
- He performs a miracle (feeds them all)!

Emotions don't have to be scary or childish. With God's help, they can be part of what guide us through life and allow us to connect with others.

Something to Think About:

1. Which role do you find yourself in most often: someone in need, someone who sees needs, someone willing to give, or someone willing to help others? Can you give an example of each of these in your life?
2. How would you describe the role emotions have in your life? Would you say you are too emotional, too cold, or somewhere in the middle? Are there

any changes you'd like to see in your emotional life?

3. During your DTS, did you witness (or were you part of) any miraculous events? Describe one as fully as you can. What do you remember about the events and the emotions that led up to and then followed the miracle?

Action Steps:

1. Take time to make a collage or poster that deals with an issue, need, or situation in the world that stirs up your compassion. As you work on this project, ask Holy Spirit to give you insight and to show you His heart for those involved. Post what you have made in a place where you can see it.
2. How is God asking you to respond to the compassion you are feeling? Giving, going, learning more, helping, teaching others, contributing something? What is an action point for you in response to this area?

Going Deeper:

1. Research a film that deals with the topic you collaged about above. In the presence of Holy Spirit, watch the film. Pay attention to the ideas, emotions, and thoughts you experience as you do so.
2. Look for individuals, ministries, or other organizations who work to bring life into the area you are thinking about. Some days it must be hard

for them to keep pressing into their work. Is there a way you could encourage them through words, actions, giving, or prayer?

Day 30 - Remember, Remember

Read: Mark 6:45-56

Reflection:

When I'm in a traditional classroom setting, I tend to be a quick learner; but when it comes to the deep truths about life and God, my ability to grasp a lesson and apply it to my life slows down considerably.

Thankfully God is willing to teach with patience and kindness. I went to my DTS without all the money I needed for the outreach. I wasn't used to depending on others, and I was too ashamed to ask for help. However, seizing the opportunity to show me something about His love and power, God provided for my fees in an unexpected and extravagant way (a pile of cash waiting on my pillow one day!).

Since then I have continued to see His faithfulness year after year. Even with countless gifts, the truth that God is trustworthy and dependable has been a challenging lesson for me to really learn. After receiving a brand new laptop, still in the box, as a unexpected gift, I proclaimed, "I'm never going to doubt God's love and His ability to provide EVER again!" Sadly, within a week or two, I needed something else and experienced the familiar fear that I wouldn't get what was required.

Like the disciples in the boat, freaking out as Jesus came toward them on the water, it seemed I too "had not gained any insight from the incident of the loaves." How could they be so clueless? How could I be so afraid? Hadn't we learned that God was with us and for us and we could live differently?

With their own eyes the disciples saw Jesus feed a huge crowd with one boy's lunch. They strained their muscles carrying the baskets of leftovers from that miracle. Why were they still confused? Why was it so hard for them to understand who Jesus was?

We are quite similar, the disciples and me. For them and for me it seems easy to doubt God's love. It seems easy to give in to fear and doubt. It seems easy to forget the hundreds of times God has come through for me. It's tempting to let circumstances erase all I know about Him.

At times like this, I'm grateful Jesus enters the boat and says, "Take courage, it is I, do not be afraid." Can you see Him with you now? Can you hear His words bringing peace to your heart? He is with us. Take courage and don't be afraid.

Something to Think About:

1. On a scale of one to ten, how confident are you that God will do all that He promises?
2. Are you generally someone who remembers and is thankful, or someone who struggles to remember what God has done?

3. What are you struggling to trust God with right now? Your health, a relationship, money, direction, peace? Invite Him to be with you in each situation where you need help.

Action Steps:

1. List five significant events during DTS where you encountered God. What did you discover about His character in each of these experiences?
2. Imagine you are in the boat with the disciples on that windy night. Jesus is walking towards you on the water. What does He say to you when He gets into the boat? Let Holy Spirit make this story come alive to you. Let Him comfort and encourage you with His presence.
3. Make a playlist of songs that are meaningful to you and that would help you remember who God is, especially in challenging times. Keep it somewhere you can find it when you need it.

Going Deeper:

1. Read Joshua chapter 4. This is where the people of Israel build a stone monument to remember their miraculous crossing of the Jordan River. Consider building a memorial of your own. You could use stones or anything else you like. What are the events that are significant in your history with God? How can building something like this help you to remember God and His ways?
2. Consider this sentence: "Imagine that you woke

up each day with only the things you thanked God for the day before." How much do you practice gratitude in your daily life? What would it look like for you to become someone who is more thankful and mindful of all you have received? Consider keeping a gratitude journal, either on paper or online, for the next week (or month).

Day 31 - Did You Wash Your Hands?

Read: Mark 7:1-13

Reflection:

It's hard to say if it's my personality or my upbringing, but I've never been very concerned with germs, cleanliness, or housework. I'm sure I've driven my parents and some roommates crazy over the years. I still have a lot to learn in this area, but having a high tolerance for dirt has been an asset during my years traveling the world.

Jesus didn't get drawn into a debate with the Pharisees about ritual cleansing. Instead He ignored the disciples' dirty hands and pointed out it's what's in your heart that is more important than required cleansing rituals.

Is it possible there are times in my life when my lips say the right thing, but my heart is far from God? Are there times when I appear to be worshiping God, but I'm actually more concerned with looking spiritual in front of others?

It's not only the Pharisees who put an emphasis on the wrong thing at times. I'm guilty of this too.

The idea of trying to fool God by putting on an outward show seems silly. After all, He knows what's in my heart. But if I'm honest, there are times when impressing someone else is a higher priority to me than pleasing God.

Jesus told the Pharisees they were doing the right actions, but their hearts were in the wrong place. They were more concerned with looking good before people than obeying God. It's not easy to hear those kinds of things, or to be told your efforts are going to waste. But I'm grateful we can trust God to show us what's really going on in our hearts and to point out when our motives are wrong. I want to be someone with a soft heart and a tender conscience, one that Holy Spirit can convict and correct. Let's ask Him to help us be concerned with what really matters, and not to get hung up on things that are less important.

Something to Think About:

1. Did you see or experience Christian behaviors in DTS that were new to you (styles of worship and prayer, views of leadership, customs, habits, etc.)? How did you respond to these differences?
2. Where would you say you are on the "rules and regulations scale": low, medium, or high?
3. How much weight do you put on what people think about you? How much weight do you put on what God thinks about you? How does this play out in your life?

Action Steps:

1. Think of someone you met during your DTS who lived or expressed their faith in a different way than you. Contact them to express your appreciation for what you learned from their example.
2. Take ten minutes to review your day yesterday. Mentally walk through your actions, words, and motivations—how you dressed, went through your day, talked with people, ate, shopped, spent time online, and so on. How much thought did you give to pleasing God? How much effort did you make to please people? What have you learned through your review of yesterday?

Going Deeper:

1. Study the life of David, Joseph, or Paul. Read though Bible passages concerning them. Where do you see a desire to please God? Where do you see a desire to please self? What insights can you gain from their mistakes and victories?
2. Who is someone you admire in regard to their desire to please God? Contact them and ask them to share with you about their story, and about how they have developed a lifestyle of closeness with God.

Day 32 - What Are You Doing To Take Care Of Your Inner World?

Read: Mark 7:14-23

Reflection:

In the West, we don't view food as clean or unclean in the same way that Jesus did. However, with the popularity of organic products, we see more connection between the way our food is produced and how it can impact us when we consume it. Taking care of our bodies is an important part of stewarding our lives, but what Jesus is drawing our attention to is a different aspect of our health.

At the core of being human lies the ability to choose: good from evil, honesty from deception, love from selfishness. These choices are part of our daily, hourly lives, no matter which country or time zone we're in.

From within a person comes potential for the long list Jesus gives: evil thoughts, murder, slander, pride, foolishness, and so on. These are the things Jesus is concerned about. These are what defile a person and what ruin friendships, destroy trust, and so much more—all from the inside out. More important than what you eat or don't eat, which rules you break or customs you ignore, is what you are doing to take care of your inner world: your heart.

Part of belonging to Christ is letting God have access to your deepest self. God sees your heart. He knows the state of your inner life. He has all the information about who you are. What He's longing for is your invitation to come in, dwell with you, and teach you how to follow Him.

So often I have felt pressure to sort out my deepest motives, desires, joys, and pains on my own. I do my best to act like I have everything together. Especially when I am far from it. Where did I get the idea it's all up to me?

When I can't be who I want to be, when I feel defiled or ruined, when my inner world is not the perfection I hope it to be… God is with me. I don't have to fix myself on my own. I don't have to pretend with God. He knows it all. He promises to make us new, and to show us what abundant life is about.

Let's let Him in, for the joy of knowing Him more, and let's ask Him to shine light on any areas that need it.

Something to Think About:

1. What about this passage is encouraging to you?
2. What about it is confusing or challenging?
3. What are the things in your inner world you try to hide or disguise from others?
4. Consider this sentence: "At the core of being human lies the ability to choose." On a day-to-day basis, how aware are you of the significance of your God-given ability to choose? Do you feel free to make choices, or do you feel pressured/forced in certain directions? Is there anything about your ability to choose that you'd like to change or strengthen?

Action Steps:

1. In this passage, Jesus lists thirteen different things that can come out of a person's heart. Take time in the next days to go over the list and reflect on the state of your heart. Is there anything you'd like to address or any changes you'd like to make? Consider talking and praying with a friend about the topic of a clean heart and God's promise to be with us.
2. Take a piece of blank paper:

- On one side, list/describe your outer self. What do people see when they look at you? How do you want people to think of you?
- On the other side of the paper, describe your inner world. What things about yourself and your story do you keep to yourself?
- Once you've written on both sides of the paper, take some time to talk with God about what you've written and what you've noticed.

Going Deeper:

1. Check out thebibleproject.com. This website is full of great videos explaining key themes from Scripture, linked with podcasts and studies. Consider watching the video called *The Law* as it ties together the Hebrew understanding of sin and morality which Jesus talks about so often and addresses in today's reading.
2. Go to YouTube and listen to Andrew Peterson

sing "Be Kind to Yourself." Close your eyes and listen as if Jesus were singing this to you. Write down what He says through this song and remind yourself throughout the week of His thoughts. Repeat whenever necessary.

Day 33 - The Woman Who Kept On Asking

Read: Mark 7:24-30

Reflection:

Fear and greed are two very powerful motivators in life. Every day there are hundreds of things that could go wrong in life and hundreds of things to worry about.

What if there isn't enough cake for *me*?

What if they lose *my* luggage?

What if *my* gift isn't as nice as hers?

You can easily imagine the possibility of failure, rejection, or not getting what you need in every situation: a job interview, an award at school, an invitation to a party, or pizza at lunch.

The woman in this passage had many obstacles keeping her from Jesus. He could have rejected her for her foreign language, foreign culture, and foreign religion. Everyone expected Jesus to ignore her, yet she took a risk to ask for His help anyway. She expected to receive something good from Jesus. She was bold and direct in her request. She "argued" with Jesus, not giving up until He answered her.

And of course, Jesus paid attention to her need and generously answered her request. She returned home to discover that her daughter had been healed. Rather than making her jump through hoops or point out all that could have disqualified her from His notice, Jesus applauded her answer. He used this interaction to reveal how the Christ had come to extend God's kingdom to *all* tribes and nations.

This woman inspires me. Based on the tiny bit she knew of Jesus's kindness and power she bravely asked for help. And if she, who had so many barriers between herself and God could hope in God's goodness and love, how much more can we have hope?

You don't have to convince God to care about you – He already does! He knows your needs and your wants. You can ask for His help without shame or fear. Instead of letting fear keep you from Him, let His goodness and love draw you closer, especially in times when you need it the most.

Something to Think About:

1. Are you afraid to ask God for some things in your life right now? Where do you think that fear might come from?
2. What are you worried or anxious about right now?
3. Do you tend to see God more as generous or as

stingy (giving only the crumbs)? Where do you think this view might come from?

Action Steps:

1. Make a list of your current needs and hopes. Think about your immediate needs and those of others you know. Imagine yourself before Jesus, like this woman was. Ask Him for the things you need. Perhaps He will have some questions or comments for you as you bring these needs to Him. Enter into a conversation with Jesus about the things you are asking for. Write down what He says to you about them.
2. Check out the website www.freerice.com, where you can test your knowledge of art, chemistry, geography, and many other subjects. For every correct answer, Freerice.com donates ten grains of rice to the hungry through the United Nations World Food Programme. How cool!

Going Deeper:

1. Read Matthew 7:7-11. What is Jesus trying to teach us in this passage about prayer and about God's character? Write a paragraph reflecting on what you can learn about God through this passage.
2. There are dozens of videos on YouTube about the story of Jesus with the Syrophoenician woman. Watch a few and see if you can learn a bit more

about the cultural and social significance of this interaction.

Day 34 - He Is Still Doing All Things Well

Read: Mark 7:31-37

Reflection:

This statement, "He has done all things well," is one of the best summaries I've heard of the life of Jesus. It was said by those who brought a deaf and mute man to Jesus for healing, and who knew He'd multiplied fish and bread, explained difficult teachings, shown compassion and mercy to the unlikely, and started many conversations about what it means to love God.

There was a consistency to the way Jesus lived. What He said and how He treated people fit together without contradiction. He was both wise and courageous. He wasn't afraid to rock the boat, and He wasn't worried if people didn't see things the way He did. At times crowds would gather around Him and then go away. People would believe, and then desert Him. Some would oppose Him, then decide to follow. There was a lot of drama!

It makes sense there was drama around Jesus. The same drama exists today. We all have questions, perceptions, misconceptions, and fears to sort through. What convinces one person won't make a dent in the doubts of another.

Each of us is in a process of discovery—about God, self, calling, and more.

When you get home from DTS, it's easy to see DTS as the solution for everyone. Got relationship problems? Go to DTS. Looking for a career path? Go to DTS. Need healing from difficult situations? Go to DTS. Struggling in your faith? Go to DTS.

Wanting people to have a life-changing experience is great. Wanting them to encounter the truth and beauty of Jesus is wonderful. What's difficult, however, is when you feel the pressure to recreate the experience of DTS or to recruit all of your friends to missions! It's difficult because *it's not your job*.

In DTS we learned it is Jesus who brings lasting change. He is the one to point people to. He is the one who forgives and transforms. His hopes and plans for each life are so much better than we could imagine or orchestrate.

So now that you're back home, tell your stories. Talk about how great Jesus is. Joyfully describe what you've learned and the healing you've experienced. Let people see Jesus at work in your life.

Keep your eyes on Him and keep learning from Him. Invite your friends to share their stories with you. Ask others about what God has been doing in your hometown. Encourage each other in your faith.

Together let's express wonder and gratitude to our great Jesus, the One who *still* does all things well.

Something to Think About:

1. What are the things from DTS you most wish your friends could experience or discover?
2. Since you've returned from DTS, have you felt any pressure to convince, change, or recruit people who are close to you? Where do you think this pressure is coming from?
3. In what ways have you been able to point people to Jesus since you've been back home?

Action Steps:

1. Take some time to think about the way God worked in and around you during DTS. Consider the phrase, "He does all things well," and journal or make a list about ways you saw the beauty and goodness of Jesus.
2. Keeping in mind it's not your responsibility to fix, change, or convince anyone about Jesus, prayerfully consider who in your life you could invite to join you in something you are doing, such as attending church, going to Bible study, participating in a mission trip, etc.

Going Deeper:

1. Do you have plans to attend or participate in any events, groups, seminars, or trips in the future to strengthen your faith? If not, research some of the opportunities available to you.

2. Consider areas of your faith life where you are strong and want to grow even more (evangelism, prayer, worship, service, etc.), or areas where you feel weak and would like to be strengthened. Ask a mentor or friend for recommendations about books, Bible studies or courses that could be beneficial.

Day 35 - Sunday Reflection

This week we considered the role of emotions in life and noticed how Jesus was aware of and responsive to His emotions. We remembered how difficult it can be to hold on to the experiences we have had with God; we need to be reminded over and over again that He cares for us and our needs. We were reminded how easy it is to focus our attention on outward actions rather than on what's going on in our heart, and about the importance of taking care of our inner world. We were encouraged to come to God with our needs and requests, knowing His care for us is genuine.

Sabbath Review: Week Five

1. Connection. In the past week, who have you connected with? Think about family members, roommates, friends from DTS, people at church, work or school friends. How did you feel about the quality of the time you spent together? How well did you listen? Is there anything that could have made the time together better?

For the coming week, consider your skills as a listener. How would you rate your listening skills? Do you interrupt people, or do you let them finish their sentences? Do you rush to speak, or do you leave space in conversations for others? Try to listen well this week.

2. Service and Generosity. In what ways have you expressed a heart of service and generosity this week? Being willing to serve is a great way to express gratitude and love to others. Service and generosity can look like washing the dishes, taking out the garbage, giving someone a ride somewhere, or asking someone about their day and listening with your full attention. Service and generosity can look like colouring with a child, calling your grandma to say "hello," letting someone ahead of you in the grocery line, or letting someone else decide which movie to watch.

For the coming week, think about creative ways you could be generous with your belongings. Could you give some thing or some money to another person? Ask Holy Spirit for His guidance in this.

3. Self-care. How have you been taking care of yourself this week? Have you been getting enough sleep? Are you eating well? Are you drinking enough water? What are you doing for exercise? Have you made time for "play," for things you find truly enjoyable: things so fun for you that you lose track of time when doing them? (This could be reading, sports, crafting, hanging out with friends, you name it.)

For the coming week, think about what beautiful things are in your living space. Do you have any photos, paintings, or pictures where you live? Are there any flowers or plants? Is your room comfortable and inviting? What could do to change or beautify your space?

4. Spiritual Life. In what ways have you been able to connect with God this week? Where have you sensed His presence as you go about your daily life? Which habits (such as reading Scripture, worship, prayer, Bible study, etc.) have you been able to engage in? What do you sense God is saying to you these days? In what ways do you sense His encouragement and affirmation of you as His child?

For the coming week, choose a favourite psalm. Write it out and place it somewhere you will see it. Read it every day this week and take some time to meditate on what it is saying.

Week Six

Day 36 - That Annoying Song Stuck In My Head

Read: Mark 8:1-21

Reflection:

YOU KNOW that moment when a catchy tune or nursery rhyme gets stuck in your brain and starts to make you go crazy? I've discovered the best way to get it out of my head is to replace it with something else – hopefully something less irritating. Isn't it interesting how the mind can get stuck on repeat? It is a great thing when truth is circulating through our thoughts, but when lies and fears won't go away, it's even more irritating than an '80s pop song.

Like the disciples in this passage, we can obsess about what we forgot, what we don't have, all the mistakes we've made, what others have done to hurt us, and all we're missing out on. This can become a cycle of blame, anger, shame, and grumpiness:

Why didn't you bring the bread?

I thought you were going to bring it.

No one asked me to.

It wasn't my turn.

Jesus doesn't scold His friends for forgetting to bring bread. He wasn't even talking about bread. But, noticing a teachable moment and how fixated they were on bread, he starts to recount the miraculous meals they've had. Jesus' questions steer the disciples back to thinking about who He is and what they've seen Him do in the past.

Sometimes the only way to get *that* annoying song out of your head is deciding to sing a different one. Sometimes the only way to get over our fear, worry, or guilt is to replace those thoughts with gratitude, praise, and reminders of who Jesus is.

Today, instead of thinking about all that you don't have and all that could go wrong, ask Holy Spirit to help you remember all God has given you. Recount the ways you have seen His power in your life.

Trust me, it's a much better song.

Something to Think About:

1. Are there things in your life right now that are stirring up fear, anxiety, shame, or anger? Take a moment to identify them and bring them to God.
2. Do you know anyone who could be a role model

for you in the area of gratitude, thankfulness, and joy? What does it feel like to be around him/her?

3. What's the "spiritual tune" running around inside of your head today? Is it a song of truth and life, or one of blame, failure, or anger? Ask Jesus to show you the truth in the situation and what He's singing over you right now.

Action Steps:

1. Make a list of ten things that you are thankful for, wherever you are today.
2. Think about the days and weeks since DTS ended. Consider all the ways that God has shown Himself to you during that time. Let the amazingly good song of God's kindness and power fill your mind with His presence and joy.

Going Deeper:

1. Take some time to look back over your DTS journal or class notes. What are some of the lessons and truths God taught you during DTS? How can those lessons apply to your life today?
2. Look over some photos from your DTS. Consider how most of the people in those photos were strangers a short time ago, but have now become dear friends. Think about how much you changed during DTS and how you saw your classmates change. How can what you experienced through these relationships bring you hope for the future? What reminders do you have

of God's ability to work in your life in each season and situation?

Day 37 - The Gift of Brutal Honesty

Read: Mark 8:22-38

Reflection:

Can you imagine how horrible it must have been on that day to be Peter and to be rebuked by Jesus? It's one thing to be told that you're *sort of* off track, but to be told that you are getting in the way of God and are on the side of the devil is something else!

I would have crawled under a rock.

However, there's something amazing about friends and leaders who are willing to be brutally honest with you. Once he got over the shock of being called out by Jesus, perhaps Peter could appreciate the truth Jesus spoke. He certainly would remember what Jesus said that day.

I worked as an executive assistant for a couple of years. One thing I appreciated about my boss was her honesty. Early in my employment, I'd sensed some tension coming from her and felt insecure about it. *Had I done something wrong? What was she expecting from me? How could I keep her happy?* I cautiously entered her office one morning and, in a moment of boldness, I asked her about it. She put down her pen, looked at me, and said, "Tanya, when I'm upset with you or your performance, I will tell you directly. Unless I do that, please assume I'm happy with you and you're doing great."

I felt relaxed and secure once again. I knew what to expect.

Now, when I'm leading others, I give them the same speech she gave me.

So, as Peter crawled out from under his rock of shame, what lessons did he learn from Jesus's words that day? Jesus didn't gloss things over. He was clear and direct. If you want to follow Me, you have to give up *everything*. If you try to save your life, you will *lose* it. If you're ashamed of Me, I will be ashamed of you.

Following Christ requires a complete turn-around from a self-centered life, and many people refuse to go there. Jesus tells us that following Him requires different priorities:

Your soul is more valuable than the entire world.

God's approval is more desirable than the approval of others.

To save your life you must give it into the hands of God.

I'm grateful for the clear, honest words of Christ. Because He was so honest with Peter, we can trust He will be honest with us as well. When we get confused about what is important, when we aren't sure who to look to for approval, when we aren't sure how to invest our lives, we can trust Holy Spirit to honestly show us the way forward.

Something to Think About:

1. Do you have people in your life who are "brutally" honest with you?

2. What does it feel like when you aren't sure where you stand in a friendship?
3. Would you prefer brutal honesty or some degree of uncertainty in a relationship? What leads you to choose one over the other?

Action Steps:

1. Take ten minutes to journal or draw a response to this question: "Who is Jesus?"
2. Who is Jesus for you today? How can you share Him—make Him alive—in your life today?
3. Imagine you were introducing Jesus as the guest speaker at a DTS. How would you prepare the class for His week?

Going Deeper:

1. Go to thebibleproject.com and watch the video giving an overview of the book of Mark.
2. Watch the short video "Something More," about the life of Christ, at movingworks.org.

Day 38 - Tell Me That Story Again

Read: Mark 9:1-13

Reflection:

Compared to "normal life," DTS is full of mind-blowing, mountain-top experiences. When you hear students giving reports about DTS outreach you quickly lose count of the times they say "amazing," "awesome," "incredible," and so on. We don't have a big enough vocabulary to express all we have seen and experienced.

In today's reading, Jesus takes his closest friends up the mountain for an encounter they didn't understand and weren't sure how to describe. Their teacher, Jesus, starts glowing with supernatural light. They see dead prophets in the flesh, and they hear God's voice from a cloud. They'd seen Jesus do amazing things before, but nothing compared to this! What did it all mean?

When they ask Him about it, Jesus swears them to secrecy. They aren't to say a word about what happened until He rises from the dead. Those instructions add to their confusion.

But Jesus knows what He's doing. What they saw up on the mountain will stick in their minds. When they don't know what to hold on to, they will be able to hold on to that extraordinary day. These men will face many difficult moments between the Transfiguration and the crucifixion, and then between the crucifixion and the rest of their lives. They will need every story, every memory, and every reminder they have that God is alive and active.

One thing that makes DTS powerful and life-changing is being part of God's story. First, you hear about God, then you experience God. You see Him at work around you. You don't always understand it, nor can you always describe what happened, but you've experienced God. You know something has changed. You know you are part of something bigger than yourself. These incredible stories give you something to hold on to when the challenges of life drag you down.

Even after twenty-plus years of following Christ, there are times when I doubt God's power. I get confused. I feel discouraged. There are days I wonder, "Have I simply made all of this up? Is Jesus real? Maybe it's all a big coincidence."

Can you relate?

In my times of doubt and confusion I am grateful for the testimony of others. Can you imagine how many times Peter, James, and John retold the story of that day on the mountain? What a gift it is to remember what God has done for others!

I don't know if I'll ever hear God's audible voice or see something like they did on the mountain, but I need to hear how others have experienced Jesus. How can you encourage others with your stories today?

Something to Think About:

1. What "miraculous" encounters have you had with Jesus? How did you respond at the time?
2. What things about Jesus are confusing to you still?
3. Do you have any friends who don't get what you are talking about when it comes to Jesus? How does that make you feel?

Action Steps:

1. Email a friend/DTS classmate today and ask them to tell you how Jesus is at work in their life these days. Share your own experience of how Jesus is at work in you.
2. How could you be more intentional about sharing your God stories with others and hearing from others about what God is doing in them? Building these types of habits into your life before times of confusion or crisis can help you to stay strong and spiritually healthy.
3. Imagine you are overhearing a conversation between the Father and Jesus. Based on verse 7, what do you think it might sound like? Write out what you think they would say to each other.

Going Deeper:

1. Read one of these books about how those from the past have experienced Jesus:

- *Foxe's Book of Martyrs*
- *Jesus Freaks* by DC Talk
- *The Heavenly Man* by Brother Yun
- A Christian biography: Amy Carmichael, Mother Teresa, etc.

Day 39 - Confused and Afraid

Read: Mark 9:14-32

Reflection:

There have been days when I've spent my entire devotional time with a wrinkled forehead—confused and bothered. Isn't the Bible supposed to be easy to understand, simple to explain, and full of great advice for every situation?

The reading from today is one of those confusing passages. It tells us about a boy so sick no doctor could cure him. We read of a father desperate to get help. Teachers are arguing about what is going on. Disciples are confused and afraid. Curious bystanders are calling out comments from the sidelines.

Can you relate to any of these characters? When's the last time you felt confusion or fear or hopelessness or boldness or curiosity about something happening around you? Have you looked in your heart and seen belief and unbelief there at the same time?

I know what it feels like to be stretched between hope and fear, or confidence and doubt. I live there a lot more often than I thought I would. Tension and questions are a big part of life. Without them we'd miss the chance to wrestle with ideas and search for truth. There's no shame in being in a place of wrestling or confusion or waiting for help.

I am so impressed by the honesty of the father. He presented both his belief and unbelief before Jesus and asked for help. Jesus didn't scold him for lack of faith or tell him to try harder in the future.

This reminds me our life of faith isn't primarily about trying hard to think or to believe the correct things. Following Jesus is about looking to Him, no matter what state we are in emotionally or mentally. Our faith is not in an *idea* but in a *person:* Jesus. He is the one who grows our faith. He helps us with our unbelief—and with everything else, for that matter.

Whether you feel it today or not, days will come when you will struggle to be confident and hopeful. Instead of getting down on yourself for being a failure or not trying hard enough, perhaps the words of this dad can inspire you. Whether your belief is strong, weak, shaky, under attack, falling to pieces, or in need of attention, you can be completely honest with Jesus about what you think and feel. He wants to help.

Something to Think About:

1. What are the things in your life right now that you are confused about?
2. In what ways can you relate to the father's statement, "I believe; help my unbelief"?
3. Are there situations in life currently where it seems your prayers are not being answered? How do you feel about this?

Action Steps:

1. Take some time to journal about your habits and

ways of dealing with difficult situations. Are you someone who avoids situations you can't fix? Someone who keeps pushing for resolution? How healthy would you say your approach is? Would you like to change anything about the way you deal with problems and challenges?

2. Are you familiar with the distinction between a *problem* and a *dilemma*? A problem refers to a difficulty that must be dealt with or fixed, while a dilemma refers to a situation that can only be managed, not solved. What difference could it make for you to redefine some of the *problems* in your life as *dilemmas?*

Going Deeper:

1. Do you have someone in your life who is able to listen and provide support regarding difficult situations that don't have a solution? Have a conversation with him/her about some of these difficult topics. If you don't have a relationship like this, consider talking with a friend about how you could support each other in dealing with situations that don't have a solution.
2. Read *Desiring God's Will* by David G. Benner, a short book exploring the important difference between trying hard(er) to love God and surrendering to Him in trust and hope.

Day 40 - A Modern Cup of Cold Water

Read: Mark 9:33-41

Reflection:

Once, on outreach in a big city, I got sick and ended up at the hospital by myself, getting treatment for a painful (and nasty-looking) infection on my legs. Sitting in the Emergency Room, scared and freaked out, I couldn't hold back my tears. I wasn't sure how I would pay the doctor's bill, and, to be honest, I didn't even know how to get back to the church where my team was staying. The nurse noticed my tears, gave me a hug, and treated me so gently. Her kindness made a huge impression on me.

Giving someone a cup of water is a basic way to show hospitality. It's a sign that you notice the person and you consider them worthy of your time and effort. A cup of water is not impressive or exotic, but when you're thirsty it's amazingly important.

Imagine if all the Christians in the world were willing "to give cups of water" to those who needed it. What if we did simple acts of kindness each day? What if, instead of getting worked up and angry about theological or political arguments, we looked for opportunities to be kind? What if we stopped worrying about how to be the best or greatest and instead looked for ways to put other people before ourselves?

Some days I make a point to pray, *God, please show me someone who needs my help*. There are days when this prayer is answered. One day I carried a woman's suitcase down the stairs in the subway. I helped a mom and baby board an airplane with all their bags. One day I gave up my seat on the bus. These are small things. Not very impressive, perhaps a modern equivalent of a cup of cold water, but it feels good to be on the giving end.

Something to Think About:

1. In what ways were you a recipient of hospitality and kindness on your DTS outreach? How did this impact you?
2. What do you think Jesus is trying to get at in verses 39-41?
3. How do you respond to people who are doing things "in Jesus' name" that you don't agree with?

Action Steps:

1. Ask God for an opportunity *today* to show kindness to someone you don't know. What will you have to change in your life in order to make space for this kind of service?
2. When was the last time you experienced the kindness and generosity of a stranger? How did you feel when this happened? Share that story with someone you know.
3. What service needs exist around you? Consider picking up a bag full of garbage in your neighbourhood, shoveling someone's sidewalk, raking leaves, or washing the dishes.

Going Deeper:

1. Is there a certain theology, religion, or social group that easily provokes anger in you? What could you do to learn more about the people who are part of that group? Consider reading a book, watching a film, or talking to someone different than you and let God show you His heart for them.
2. Watch the short film "Follower" on movingworks.org about a woman who responds to God's leading to minister to the Deaf community.

Day 41 - Walking the Bumpy Sidewalk

Read: Mark 9:42-50

Reflection:

The sidewalk near my apartment is made of many different surfaces. Some parts are paved, some are brick, some are cobblestone. Some parts are bumpy and broken up by tree roots growing under the sidewalk. A simple walk can be treacherous–especially when it's dark or rainy, or when I'm not really paying attention.

As the days go by, I've learned where the bumpy parts are. Usually, I remember where I need to pay attention, and when it's easier to simply cross the street.

Jesus doesn't mention sidewalks, but He talks a lot about stumbling. What's interesting to me about stumbling is that you can usually avoid it if you focus on what you're doing.

In DTS, there were only so many "sidewalks" you could go down. Your options were limited—who to hang out with, where to go, what to do. Most likely you were so busy with worship nights, adventures, and outreaches that there was little time left for stumbling around.

Now that DTS is over and you're back home, it's important to pay more attention to the environment around you. I've noticed there are certain habits, people, shows, places, and even songs that have more of an effect on me than I'd like. I need to be extra attentive to my thoughts, actions, and responses when I'm in these situations.

Jesus makes a connection between our hands and eyes and feet and the impact they have on others. What I do and say influences others in ways I can't necessarily predict or control. My life isn't just about me doing what I like and filling my time with stuff I enjoy. Even if I'm not stumbling myself, there's the possibility I could cause others to stumble! Jesus takes this very seriously indeed.

Life is about more than walking down a sidewalk and not falling over. We've got places to go and things to do. There are other things to spend our energy on! Wouldn't it be a shame if I had to spend all my time looking down, fearful of what might happen to me? Taking time to notice obstacles in the road, even being willing to change my path to avoid them, doesn't steal my freedom. Being aware of what could trip me up or hurt someone else actually gives me more freedom to enjoy my walk and arrive at my destination with energy to spare.

Something to Think About:

1. What are some of the places, activities, or relationships in your life that have potential to make you stumble? What is your normal approach to these things?
2. What parts of your life (words, actions, attitudes) do you think have the most influence on the people around you?
3. What do you think Jesus is trying to get at with His bold statements about plucking out an eye and cutting off a hand?

Action Steps:

1. Go for a thirty-minute walk outside. For at least part of the time, walk somewhere that's not your regular route. Pay attention to the road or path you are walking on. What do you notice about it? How much effort does it take to walk without stumbling?
2. In order to become more aware of "the sidewalk" of your life, keep a log of the people, places, and activities in your life and how they influence you. Take a paper and divide it into two columns. Label one side "smooth walking" and the other side "potential for stumbling." Make some notes each day about what strengthens you in your walk with God and what makes it difficult for you to be the person you want to be.

Going Deeper:

1. It is easier to walk a difficult path in the light than in the dark. What places in your mind or emotions have you kept hidden? Begin the journey of bringing these places "into the light" by talking to God about them. Give Him the opportunity to bring someone into your life who would listen and help you experience more freedom. You don't have to walk this path alone.
2. Consider watching a film or reading something about *The Camino de Santiago*, such as the 2010 film called *The Way*. The Camino de Santiago is an ancient pilgrimage route beginning in various places in Europe and ending in northwestern Spain. There is a lot we can learn about walking, stumbling, and paying attention from those who have taken this 500-mile journey.

Day 42 - Sunday Reflection

This week we considered how to replace the song of guilt, shame, and fear with a song about who God is and how He cares for us. We looked at Jesus' rebuke of Peter and saw the value of friends who will be completely honest with us. We remembered how important it is to hear the stories of what God has done in the lives of others. We reflected on the tension between belief and unbelief that exists in every heart and tried to give ourselves permission to be honest about the questions we have. Our faith isn't primarily about ideas but rather resides in a person—Jesus

—who is alive and available. We talked about ways we've received hospitality and shown hospitality to others, and we ended the week thinking about what it means to walk through life with enough awareness to avoid unnecessary stumbling.

Sabbath Review: Week Six

1. Connection. In the past week, who have you connected with? Think about family members, roommates, friends from DTS, people at church, work or school friends. How did you feel about the quality of the time you spent together? How well did you listen? Is there anything that could have made the time together better?

For the coming week, do a little research to see who has a birthday in the coming week or two. Buy a card and send it to them.

2. Service and Generosity. In what ways have you expressed a heart of service and generosity this week? Being willing to serve is a great way to express gratitude and love to others. Service and generosity can look like washing the dishes, taking out the garbage, giving someone a ride somewhere, or asking someone about their day and listening with your full attention. Service and generosity can look like colouring with a child, calling your grandma to say "hello," letting someone ahead of you in the grocery line, or letting someone else decide which movie to watch.

For the coming week, invite someone you don't know well to a meal or for coffee with you.

3. Self-care. How have you been taking care of yourself this week? Have you been getting enough sleep? Are you eating well? Are you drinking enough water? What are you doing for exercise? Have you made time for "play," for things you find truly enjoyable: things so fun for you that you lose track of time when doing them? (This could be reading, sports, crafting, hanging out with friends, you name it.)

For the coming week, make yourself a *gratitude jar* out of whatever container you can find. Each day, week, or however often works for you, write down the date and something you are grateful for, and put it in the jar. As often as necessary, open the jar and review what you have to be grateful for.

4. Spiritual Life. In what ways have you been able to connect with God this week? Where have you sensed His presence as you go about your daily life? Which habits (such as reading Scripture, worship, prayer, Bible study, etc.) have you been able to engage in? What do you sense God is saying to you these days? In what ways do you sense His encouragement and affirmation of you as His child?

For the coming week, find the painting *The Incredulity of Saint Thomas* by Caravaggio online and take time to meditate on it, paying attention to the facial expressions, the light and dark, and the overall theme of the painting.

Week Seven

Day 43 - Relationships Matter To God

Read: Mark 10:1-12

Reflection:

DURING MY DTS, I had a crush on pretty much every single guy in the school. For the first time in my life, I was around men who loved God and included Him in their relationships. I wasn't used to being treated with kindness and respect.

Being in a setting where romantic relationships were off the table gave me freedom to develop friendships with many interesting people. Before going to DTS, I'd been trained to see every guy as a potential date. I was used to quickly judging people as "my type" or "not my type." I had a lot to learn about relating well.

In DTS, you had space to talk about relationships. You were in a safe environment, surrounded by godly friends and leaders. You understood that relationships didn't have to be instantly romantic or physical. Friendships had a place to grow.

But now you're swimming in a different pond. The contrast between healthy and unhealthy relating can be disorienting. The familiar pressure to date, find a partner, or hook up is in your face once again. What are you going to do about it? Where can you find the support you need? How can you take all you've learned in DTS and truly live it?

In a world that's incredibly confused about love, relationships, and sexuality, you don't have to live in fear and anxiety. You've learned so much about honesty, kindness, and courage. You've grown in freedom. You've forgiven others and been forgiven. You're learning to give and receive love, and that's not a small thing. Keep it up.

Your relationships, sexuality, and desires are incredibly important to God. They aren't unspiritual or beneath Him. Learning to relate in healthy ways is worthy of your time and effort but you can't do it alone. You need a community to encourage you, watch out for you, coach you, pray with you, and remind you of God's perspective on relationships.

Marriage is a gift from God. Divorce is a painful tragedy. You may not be thinking about a relationship or marriage right now, but relationships matter; and, with God's help, we can be men and women who love well.

Something to Think About:

1. In what ways did your view of romantic relationships change during DTS?
2. What did you learn, or how did you grow, during DTS in regard to developing a healthy view of relationships?
3. What are the areas in your current situation you'd like to adjust when it comes to building healthy relationships with others (romantic and non-romantic)?

Action Steps:

1. If you don't already have one, consider finding an accountability partner you could meet with on a regular basis to talk and pray about healthy relationships, sexuality, and friendships.
2. If you don't already have one, consider the possibility of getting a mentor—an older person or married couple who could pray for you and support you in your relationships.
3. Do you know someone who's going through a break up, separation, or divorce? Make the effort to be a friend to him or her in a practical way.
4. If your DTS leader and/or staff were married, pray for these marriages. If your pastor is married, pray for his/her marriage to be strengthened.

Going Deeper:

1. Check out the website truelovedates.com for articles and resources about dating, relationships, and faith.
2. If you're married, make it a priority to attend a couples retreat or workshop in the next few months.
3. If you are an adult child of divorce, consider reading the book I wrote about this topic, *Come Home Laughing*. It's available on Amazon.
4. Broken relationships, family issues, and abuse are just a few examples of what can get in the way of healthy relationship patterns. If you struggling to connect with people in healthy ways, you may want to consider meeting with a pastor or counselor. Going to counseling was one of my best decisions, and one I wished I'd made much earlier than I did.
5. Consider reading one of these books about healthy relationships:

- *Relationships: The Key to Love, Sex, and Everything Else* by Dean Sherman
- *Boundaries in Dating* by Henry Cloud and John Townsend
- *True Love Dates* by Deborah Fileta
- *Love, Sex, and Lasting Relationships* by Chip Ingram
- *Real Sex* by Lauren Winner
- *The Mystery of Marriage* by Mike Mason

Day 44 - A Return To Childhood

Read: Mark 10:13-16

Reflection:

The disciples have so much to learn. Poor guys. I feel sorry for them when I read all the hare-brained things they do and say. Today's blunder is one of the worst. Everyone who's been to Sunday school knows "Jesus loves the little children"!

Before I criticize them too much, I admit there are many things about Jesus I don't understand either. If I'd been "on outreach" with the disciples that day, I'd probably have been so focused on getting from Point A to Point B that I would have pushed the children away too.

We don't often see Jesus get angry, but in this situation He's indignant! Whatever plans had been on the agenda for that day got tossed out in order for Jesus to make a point about the place children have in the kingdom. Apparently Jesus wants us to learn something about faith from children.

I am not a parent, but I've noticed how children can be impulsive, affectionate, loud, and generous. Time and schedules don't rush them. They are curious, honest, and blunt. They are confident they will be taken care of.

In some ways, going on outreach is like a return to childhood. When you're in a foreign country, you are dependent on your host, taxi driver, and ultimately on God. You have to ask a lot of questions and you need to accept help. You have the opportunity to see through new eyes. You remember the beauty of cooperation and sharing. Eventually you stop trying to force things to happen. You relax and trust you will be taken care of.

And so, since we can't become children again, perhaps we can embrace the attitudes of openness, trust, and teachability instead. Could we slow down a bit and delight in the small things just like a child does? Could we surrender our need to control *every*thing? Could we let Jesus embrace us, as we are, and receive the kingdom life He offers so freely? Wanna try?

Something to Think About:

1. What connection do you see between childlikeness and being in a different culture for the first time?
2. How did you respond to the dependence you experienced on outreach? Were you continually frustrated with not being able to do things on your own, or were you able to embrace needing the help of others?
3. Which "childlike" attitude is God inviting you to embrace today?

Action Steps:

1. Look for something childlike you could do today (swing at the playground, jump in a puddle, watch a caterpillar) and then go for it. After you're finished, reflect on the experience and what it was like to be in the moment.
2. Offer to babysit for a family.

3. Donate $20 to a ministry helping at-risk children.

Going Deeper:

1. Are you someone who is interested in working with children or youth in the future? If so, take some time to research opportunities for service in your church or community. What courses or training could you get to help prepare you for what's ahead?
2. Is there a person from your DTS working with youth who needs your prayers or financial support? Contact them to see what needs they have. Ask Holy Spirit how you can encourage them in what they are doing.

Day 45 - What You've Given Up, What You'll Receive, What You Have Right Now

Read: Mark 10:17-31

Reflection:

Every December I spend a couple days reviewing the past twelve months—what's happened, where I've been, significant events and experiences. I count the flights, visits from friends, completed projects, ways I've grown, accomplishments, and so on. I squeeze everything I can into one double-page in my journal to create an overview of the year.

Looking at a year from that perspective shrinks the bumps and scratches of daily life into proper size. But, in my less wise moments, I feel a lot like the rich young ruler and the disciples, anxious to figure out what the future holds and wondering if I'll be okay. The questions they asked are good questions. What's wrong with wanting to know if we've done enough, if we've followed the rules, if we'll be rewarded for our efforts?

Jesus' replies to their questions aren't totally straightforward. Yes, the disciples will receive something for all they've given up for His sake. They will receive a lot! Job, home, parents, children, and so on. Jesus doesn't make light of what they have sacrificed or what they will be given, but it's not all roses and moonlight. There's persecution too.

Life always involves choices and sacrifices. Christian or not, missionary or not, YWAMer or not, we all have to make choices and sacrifices, and they aren't easy decisions. Some people focus on what they've given up—the people they've said goodbye to and the opportunities they've turned down. Others dream continually about what the future might hold—that promise of a hundredfold friends and houses.

But when you live with your focus on what you've lost or what you might gain, it's almost impossible to notice what you've been given right now. Day by day, month by month, a year at a time, God gives us what we need to follow Him. There's nothing wrong with missing what you've given up or dreaming of what could happen, but as you focus on His faithfulness, you worry less about what might be waiting around the corner. And you just might discover more space in your heart and mind to appreciate what's in front of you today.

Something to Think About:

1. Are you someone who focuses more on what's happened in the past or on what might happen in the future?
2. What are some of the choices or sacrifices you are contemplating in this season? What are some of your fears or hopes related to these decisions?
3. Are there any things you've given up for God that you are still "holding on to"?

Action Steps:

1. Take time to review the last six months or last year of your life. Try to fit it all on one big paper for the sake of perspective. What are the significant events, experiences, and landmarks of each month? How does looking at your life in this way give you perspective?
2. Make a list of the things you've given up or are giving up now to follow God. These things could be relationships, a home, a job, etc. Imagine these things in the palms of your hands and offer them to God, trusting Him to receive these gifts with kindness and to care for you as you live without them.

Going Deeper:

1. Get in touch with someone who is serving God outside their home country (could be a missionary from your church, a fellow YWAMer, a friend teaching English abroad). Ask about what is going well and what is difficult. Pray for this person in the areas that are difficult. Could you send a piece of mail or a care package?
2. Spend some time taking stock of your belongings (or some of them). Begin by looking at the items in one drawer, your purse, or your desk. Touch or pick up an item. Think about where it came from. How did you feel when you first saw/used/wore it? Was it a gift? If so, who gave it to you? What was the occasion? If it wasn't a gift, where did you buy it? Where did the money to buy this item come from? Repeat this process for each object. Think about all the different ways God has provided for you. Thank Him for His amazing generosity.

Day 46 - It Was A Lot Easier In The Classroom!

Read: Mark 10:32-45

Reflection:

Not long after DTS, I got a job at a Canadian doughnut shop called *Tim Hortons*. It was a good job in many ways, but it tested all I'd learned about service and humility in my DTS. I had to wear a polyester uniform *and* a hairnet —how embarrassing! So often when I was at work wearing my ugly uniform and earning minimum wage, I felt invisible and unimportant. I wasn't seen or noticed for my gifts or my important role in God's kingdom.

Even though I had taken notes about humility and servanthood, and had read Bible verses about these things, I struggled to be kind to rude customers and gracious with coworkers. It was a lot easier in the DTS classroom!

What might make it better, I thought, was if the store manager were a close friend of mine. If the person who called the shots at work liked me, I might get a raise. A better uniform. Maybe I wouldn't have to take a turn scraping gum off the bottom of the tables.

I can understand why James and John took advantage of their closeness to Jesus to ask for a favor. Since Jesus was on track to be the Messiah and ruler of their nation, it wouldn't be too hard for Him to give out positions in the upcoming government, right? After all, they were His close friends and had worked with Him for years. Don't we all hope our connections with people of wealth or power might result in a few perks for us?

Jesus didn't say much about the request of James and John. I wonder if He was disappointed His friends hadn't made the connection between His example and the way He wanted them to live. He loved serving and wanted them to love serving too. Jesus came to show us a different way of leadership and life—one where it's a joy to give to others and where the role of servant is one we are eager to take.

Something to Think About:

1. Do you know any influential, famous, or rich people? If so, have you ever received something from them or hoped you'd benefit because of your connection?
2. Did you have friends or leaders in DTS who were outstanding examples of servanthood? What did you learn from them?
3. Who in your life now is as example to you of servanthood?
4. What are some of the benefits and challenges of serving? Of being served?

Action Steps:

1. Think of a five-minute, fifteen-minute, or thirty-minute "something" you could do today to serve someone else. Choose one of these activities that you can realistically do and go for it! As you do this act, thank Jesus that He is such a good example of a servant.
2. Be extra kind and affirming today to some who has a "service" job: a waitress, cashier, bus driver, etc. What can you say or do to speak life and truth to them?

Going Deeper:

1. Do a word study on "serve/servant/servanthood" in the gospels. How many times does Jesus talk about serving? What kinds of things does He say about serving?
2. Read Philippians 2:3-11. What does this passage say about Jesus' approach and attitude toward serving? What would it look like to follow in His footsteps?

Day 47 - And He Kept On Asking

Read: Mark 10:46-52

Reflection:

As a kid, I was extremely shy. A direct question would cause me to blush bright red and render me speechless. I hated being put on the spot or having to talk to strangers.

However, I had a moment of freedom during a visit to Santa one year. I'd had a lot of time to consider my request and I knew what I wanted. When I sat on Santa's knee in the shopping mall, I found the courage to ask for what I wanted. The hope of what I might receive and the excitement of that special moment were bigger than my fears.

I wonder how often the blind man, Bartimaeus, had asked

others for help. How often did he daydream about life with sight? Did he ever cry himself to sleep wishing he could be like everyone else walking down the street? How many times had he imagined the freedom that would come from being able to see?

Finally, a man who might be able to help comes to town. A rabbi with a track record for healing is close enough to hear. As soon as Bartimaeus discovers Jesus is nearby, he does what he can do; he cries out for help. Loudly. Over and over again. He asks for what he needs. When people tell him to stop asking, he refuses to shut up.

The courage and determination of this man inspire me. No one could get Bartimaeus to be quiet. He knew what he wanted, and he wasn't willing to give up until Jesus had heard him. He didn't try to earn healing or prove his goodness; he simply asked, trusting with child-like faith. He couldn't force Jesus to do anything, but he made sure his request was heard. What a great example!

Something to Think About:

1. Do you think Bartimaeus got tired of asking people for help? Why or why not?
2. If you had been there that day in the crowd, how would you have responded to Bartimaeus' yelling in the street?
3. Are you someone who quiets down when people tell you to stop, or are you someone who won't be quiet about what's important to you?
4. What are some things in your life you really need answers for?

Action Steps:

1. Make a list of the things you want Jesus to do for you. If it helps, make categories of relational, spiritual, financial, school/work, and physical. Don't be ashamed to ask Jesus for His help. He hears you.
2. Ask Holy Spirit to show you if there are things in your life you have been avoiding or ways you have been procrastinating. If He shows you anything, take at least one step toward accomplishing this thing.

Going Deeper:

1. How much thought have you given to long-term goals and plans in your life? One tool that's helped me to think about long-term plans and goals is a workbook called *A Leader's Life Purpose Workbook* by Tony Stoltzfus.
2. Sometimes I get completely overwhelmed by all that I need and all that I don't have. I feel frozen and stuck, unsure of how to move forward. If you find yourself in this place take a break and have a personal dance party. Find a tune that gets your toes tapping, shut the door to your room and get your heart pumping. If dancing isn't your thing, watch "A Pep Talk from Kid President" on YouTube. It will make you smile.

Day 48 - How Did Everything Change So Quickly?

Read: Mark 11:1-11

Reflection:

This passage is a classic example of hearing God's voice and doing what He says. The directions were so clear—enter village, find colt, untie it, bring it here, and if anyone bothers you, say these words. Tada!

And for sure, there are some days when everything in life goes as planned: guidance is clear, all your ideas are great, people laugh at your jokes, the traffic lights are green, and every item on your grocery list is on sale!

Then, there are days when nothing seems to go your way. The toast burns, cell battery dies, people misunderstand what you say, and you stub your toe running for the bus.

I much prefer the good days, and we just read about an amazing one. I hope you had some days like this during DTS. I hope you experienced times of crystal clear guidance, words of knowledge, everything turning out better than expected! I hope you saw hearts touched by God's Spirit and crowds praising the Creator God. What a privilege and joy it is to flow with the Spirit in doing the works of the kingdom!

If you've read the rest of Mark, you will know it isn't long after this remarkable day of Jesus being welcomed with palm branches and "hosannas" that the same crowd will turn against Him. Their praises will change to scornful accusation and He will be executed. How did everything shift so quickly?

Not every day is as great as "the colt and palm Sunday." We don't always get clear instruction about where to go and who to talk to. We don't always get cheers and welcome. Our prayers don't always get answered as we think they will.

Don't be discouraged when a bad day follows a great one. Ups and downs were a part of Jesus' life, and they are a part of your life too. The story isn't over yet, and God is with us.

Something to Think About:

1. Can you think about a time during DTS when things went from really good to really bad very quickly? How did you feel about that? What thoughts went through your mind when that happened?
2. If you had to rate your experience of hearing God, what percentage of the time would you say you hear "very clearly"? What percentage of the time is His voice "clear"? What percentage is it "unclear"? What about "very unclear"?
3. Was there a time on your DTS outreach when you felt like the disciples—welcomed into a city with cheers and fanfare? What was that experience like?

Action Steps:

1. Remind yourself that emotions, seasons, and people's opinions can change very quickly. Don't be discouraged next time you experience highs and lows—Jesus' disciples experienced the same thing.
2. Think about the percentages you came up with in question two above. Compare your answers with a friend or DTS classmate and talk about your experience of hearing God's voice.
3. Connect with a friend today about a situation where you would like more clarity or direction. Talk and pray together about what's going on.

Going Deeper:

1. One book I've found helpful about the topic of hearing God's voice is Brad Jersak's *Children, Can You Hear Me?* This children's book explains God's desire to speak to us and the different ways we can hear from Him. Check it out.
2. Another great book I enjoyed is Anne Lamott's *Help, Thanks, Wow: Three Essential Prayers.* What I appreciate about this book is the way she presents prayer as an appropriate response to both the challenges and the delights of life. You can find it on Amazon.

Day 49 - Sunday Reflection

This week we started out thinking about how important relationships are to God. They are not beneath Him but rather an area of life worthy of our time and effort. We considered how much we can learn about faith and living from the honesty and hope of children. We were reminded it's normal to dream about the future and wonder what's waiting for us down the road, but focusing too much on what's to come robs us of the ability to enjoy what we have in the present.

We noticed the way Jesus served others, not just to look good or get it over with, but to set an example for us to follow. We ended the week with the awareness that life is full of ups and downs, times when things are clear, and times when we are confused. The way I feel next week might be very different from what I feel now. Hold on to Him. He is trustworthy.

Sabbath Review: Week Seven

1. Connection. In the past week, who have you connected with? Think about family members, roommates, friends from DTS, people at church, work or school friends. How did you feel about the quality of the time you spent together? How well did you listen? Is there anything that could have made the time together better?

For the coming week, think of a child in your life you could spend time with or support by attending one of his/her sporting games or musical performances. Let the child know you enjoyed watching them and cheering for them.

2. Service and Generosity. In what ways have you

expressed a heart of service and generosity this week? Being willing to serve is a great way to express gratitude and love to others. Service and generosity can look like washing the dishes, taking out the garbage, giving someone a ride somewhere, or asking someone about their day and listening with your full attention. Service and generosity can look like colouring with a child, calling your grandma to say "hello," letting someone ahead of you in the grocery line, or letting someone else decide which movie to watch.

For the coming week, think about what you could do to simplify and downsize. Go through your closet, shelves, and library and consider what you could give away.

3. Self-care. How have you been taking care of yourself this week? Have you been getting enough sleep? Are you eating well? Are you drinking enough water? What are you doing for exercise? Have you made time for "play," for things you find truly enjoyable: things so fun for you that you lose track of time when doing them? (This could be reading, sports, crafting, hanging out with friends, you name it.)

For the coming week, think about the relationships in your life that *drain* you and the ones that *energize* you. Do what you can to make sure you spend time with people who build you up and bring you life.

4. Spiritual Life. In what ways have you been able to connect with God this week? Where have you sensed His presence as you go about your daily life? Which habits (such as reading Scripture, worship, prayer, Bible study, etc.) have you been able to engage in? What do you sense God is saying to you these days? In what ways do you sense His encouragement and affirmation of you as His child?

For the coming week, listen to your favourite worship album while going on a walk. Try to keep your mind from wandering to your future plans or the situations that are stressing you out. Instead, remain in the present and turn your heart toward God.

Week Eight

Day 50 - Are There Times It's Okay To Be Angry?

Read: Mark 11:12-33

Reflection:

MY DAD IS a pretty mellow guy. As a kid I don't remember seeing him get angry about many things. One benefit of his temperament was I rarely got scolded, but it left me with very few examples of how to deal with anger. I wasn't sure when it was appropriate, when it was a bad thing, or how I ought to express myself when I felt anger.

As I studied the life of Jesus during my DTS, I observed He was compassionate and even-tempered, though He had His feisty moments too. There were a few times, like this story, where He got angry and threw a fit, and I wasn't sure what to make of these outbursts. Since He was Jesus, they had to be a good thing—right?

Could it be there are times it's okay to be angry? Are there things I'm allowed to be upset about? Is it reasonable to conclude there are times when what I've seen and heard demands a raised voice and a rebuke?

A significant part of Jesus' mission on earth was to reveal God's nature and character to all nations. The anger Jesus expressed was in response to the misuse of the temple. Instead of making space for people to worship and draw near to God, the temple was being used for financial gain. God's design of the temple and the reality of the situation did not line up. The Father's love for the world was not being reflected through the people (priests and temple servants) whose role it was to represent God. I get angry about that too!

There are events, situations, and things in life that should stir up anger in you. It's okay to have strong feelings about injustice, pain, and the misuse of God's creation. Anger can point to a value which has been violated. Anger can be a positive and helpful motivator. Next time you're aware of yourself feeling angry, look to God for guidance. His Spirit lives in you. Perhaps He also feels anger about what has stirred you up.

Invite Him to show you how to respond to the anger you feel. He can handle your anger.

Something to Think About:

1. In general, how do you deal with your feelings of anger?

2. What are some things you felt angry about during your DTS?
3. What situations, events, or interactions have stirred up your anger since you've been home?
4. What issues or situations do you think God feels anger about in your community or city?

Action Steps:

1. Today, keep track of all the times during the day when you feel angry, irritated, or upset. Do you notice any patterns about what stirs you up? Is the anger you experience a righteous anger, a selfish anger, or a mixture of the two?
2. If there are things you are angry about that you can't let go of, bring them to Jesus and ask for His help. Pray with a friend about this.

Going Deeper:

1. Do a word study through the New Testament about God's anger. What do you notice about the things God feels anger about?
2. Read one of the following books to learn about healthy emotions and relationships:

- *Boundaries* or *How People Grow*, by Henry Cloud and John Townsend
- *Safe People* by Henry Cloud and John Townsend
- *Emotionally Healthy Spirituality* by Peter Scazzero

Day 51 - You Are Not An Average Citizen

Read: Mark 12:1-17

Reflection:

Even in Jesus' time, money and politics could stir up an argument faster than almost anything. Not much has changed in that regard.

Jesus was so wise in his exchange with the leaders of His day. He was able to avoid the loaded questions about taxes and governmental authority, and He used the conversation to make a profound statement about how our lives should reflect God. I never would have made a connection between paying taxes and the invitation to live out our God-designed destiny. Since we are made in God's image, our very lives belong to Him!

In many kingdoms and countries of the world, flags, pictures, and statues remind citizens whom they "serve." Since the beginning of history, rulers have understood that people need to be reminded to whom they belong—who has power over them. Loyalty to a sovereign needs to be nurtured and developed from generation to generation.

When God created the world, He didn't build a huge statue in the middle to remind people who He was. Humans themselves are to remind each other what God is like. The "job" of humanity, so to speak, is to represent God to the world. We are God's ambassadors on earth.

An ambassador is sent to a foreign nation to represent the interests and will of the ruler. The words and actions of an ambassador are to be in line with the wishes and goals of the sovereign. The promises and claims of an ambassador are backed with authority.

You are God's ambassador. You have been sent to the place where you are now. Your assignment is to represent the wishes and values of your sovereign. When you speak and act, do so in a way that would please the King. You may *look* like an average citizen, but you are not. You take His presence into every café, classroom, office building, and gym you visit.

What would it look like if we lived each day in the awareness that we have been called to reflect God to the world? The coins in your pocket bear the image of a king, queen, or president, but your life is meant to display God to everyone around you.

May God help us to live today so people can see Him clearly in us.

Something to Think About:

1. How would you describe the concept of being made in the image of God?
2. Why do you think rulers spend so much time reminding citizens of their image and position?
3. What do you think it would look like for you to reflect God to others today?

Action Steps:

1. Make a list of your involvement in each of the

seven spheres of society (family, economics, government, religion, education, communication, and celebration). What type of influence do you have in each sphere? What would it look like for you to intentionally represent God in these places?
2. Who can you think of who represents God to you clearly? Contact them today and let them know a bit about how you see God more clearly because of them.
3. Pray for your DTS classmates and yourself (as well as for those reading this devotional) to be freed from unnecessary distractions and barriers in order to reflect God's love and character to the world.

Going Deeper:

1. Watch the 6-minute video from thebibleproject.com called *Image of God.* It's about what it means to be made in God's image and how we can represent God to the world.
2. Read Ephesians 6:18-20. What can you learn from these verses about representing Christ to the world?
3. Read 2 Corinthians 5:17-20. What is God's intention for you as His representative to the world?
4. Watch *I am a missionary* on YouTube. This 4-minute video is narrated by Loren Cunningham and brings me to tears every time.

Day 52 - When Fear Steals Your Chocolates

Read: Mark 12:18-27

Reflection:

A while ago, a friend gave me a box of gourmet chocolates. I ate one and saved the rest for a day when I might need a special treat. As it turns out, I put the box on a shelf and forgot about it for months. When I discovered the box again I was delighted—it was just the kind of day to enjoy something special!

However, my joy turned to disgust in one bite. The chocolates (all organic, no preservatives) had gone rotten on the shelf. I had to spit out the chocolate and throw them all in the garbage. What a waste!

I had done such a good job anticipating a horrible day in the future when I would need fancy chocolates to cheer me up, I prevented myself from enjoying my gift. And the whole purpose of that gift was that I would be able to enjoy it! Fear stole the blessing right out from under me.

We have a God who is alive! He is more than a character in a book or a judge searching for answers to bizarre questions about a woman who just might marry seven brothers. He is dynamic, powerful, creative, and interactive. He wants to be involved with us in the present. He has things to say and blessings to share with us today. Don't let fear about all that could go wrong in the future rob you of these gifts.

Something to Think About:

1. Are you more the type who would eat all the chocolates at once, or the type who would save them for a rainy day in the future?
2. When you picture God, what image comes to mind?
3. What things do you feel God is inviting you to participate in with Him today?

Action Steps:

1. What is an activity that makes you feel like you are alive? Plan to do that activity sometime this week.
2. Make a list of your fears regarding the present and the future. Commit these situations to God, remembering He's alive, present, and active in your life. If you would like to, rip up, burn, or throw away your list as a sign that you trust God to care for you.

Going Deeper:

1. There are parts of the Bible that are just as challenging to understand and interpret today as they were for the religious leaders in Jesus' time. Check out *The SourceView Bible* and *The SphereView Bible*, which format the Bible to show who is speaking in each verse (SourceView) and which spheres of society (SphereView) are being addressed (www.sourceviewbible.com).

Day 53 - Is It Love Or Something Else?

Read: Mark 12:28-34

Reflection:

We would all agree *love* is extremely important, but that doesn't make us any less confused about it.

Where does it come from?

How do we find it?

How do we express it?

When and how should we receive it?

Is it an emotion, a choice, or both?

Do we have a say in whom we love, or who loves us?

What happens when love fades or goes bad?

In the reading today, Jesus implies that love is something over which we have control. It's not a trifle we can push to the side or some kind of add-on for when we have spare time. Love is to consume our heart, soul, mind, and strength. It is to be our first priority, our foundational motivation.

Doing something with all of yourself is never effortless. It's complex. Love involves thoughts, emotions, decisions, ideas, action, effort, and body. It is a concept and a practice, invisible and visible, internal and external. Love is to be our attitude toward God *and* people. All people.

Some days I read these instructions and feel encouraged by the simplicity. Love. Just love.

Some days all I see is a list of the ways I could go wrong. What if my heart gets it right, but my strength messes up? What if my mind knows how to love, but my soul won't get with the program? It's exhausting!

Then I stop and remind myself that loving God isn't about collecting points or proving something. It is a choice to respond to what He's done for me. It's gratitude and wonder expressed in words and actions. More than service, activities, or sacrifices, God hopes for His love to be returned by His creation.

There's a temptation to reduce faith to right actions and answers. We try to gain security through ritual and sacrifice: going to church, reading the Bible, listening to worship music, and supporting missions. In DTS we did lots of those activities, and we did them well. They were a source of life and growth for us, which is great. But as we stay busy doing the work of the kingdom, how can we be sure we don't allow these things to distract us from what's truly the most important thing—loving God?

Something to Think About:

1. Do you remember learning and talking about love during DTS? Did any of the speakers or leaders giving a definition of "love"? What did they say it was? Look through your notes or journal if you need a reminder.

2. What are some other ways people define *love*? Think about music, TV shows, movies, books, etc.
3. How can you tell if you are acting out of love or out of duty? What's the difference? In what way does the reason behind what you are doing matter?

Action Steps:

1. Take some time today to spend with the Father. Meditate on this passage and ask Him to bring you a deeper understanding of its significance.
2. Think about this quote: "Today I'm going to love God and whoever is standing in front of me." How could that apply to your life at work, school, or home?
3. Think about one thing you want for yourself, and then go and do that for someone else.

Going Deeper:

1. Take some time to creatively express *the great commandment* in a way that you could share with a new believer or non-Christian. You could write, draw, blog, or make a video.
2. I remember a conversation with a friend who said, "I believe in God and I obey God, but *loving* God doesn't really cross my mind." Make some time to check in with yourself. How are things between you and God? Are you loving God or just doing the stuff you're supposed to do?

Day 54 - She Gave Everything She Had

Read: Mark 12:35-44

Reflection:

One of the most effective ways God has discipled me over the years is through money. If you want to know what a person really loves, look at how they spend their money. Growing up I didn't have a lot of money, but I felt very attached to what I had. Whether I'd earned it or it was given to me, I held on to it very tightly. The more money I had, the safer I felt. The less money I had, the more afraid I was. I assumed everyone else felt and lived the same way.

But then, YWAM. YWAMers saw money very differently than I did. Extreme generosity. Fearless planning. Trust in God regardless of the bank balance. Willing to share. Willing to receive. It took some getting used to, that's for sure. Over and over again God was saying, "Tanya, you can trust *Me*. I'm more reliable than a big bank account."

I was at a big gathering, and it was time to take the offering. I took out my wallet to write a cheque for a certain amount. Then I felt God prompt me to add a zero to the amount. I hesitated. I could afford what I'd planned to give, but increasing my gift by ten times was an uncomfortable suggestion. I was saving for a plane ticket to Central Asia. Wouldn't it be irresponsible to give it away?

As I sat there, the thought came to mind—if I can't trust

God to provide for a plane ticket, why would I get on a plane and move to another continent? If I can't trust Him to take care of my bank account, why would I trust Him to care of my life?

I wrote the cheque with the extra zero and dropped it in the offering plate with peace in my heart. I decided to trust God to take care of me. I didn't want to miss a chance to show Him I trusted Him. No one but God knew how much I'd given or what was going on inside, but it felt wonderful to be an extravagant giver!

I wonder what went through the mind of the widow Jesus saw that day. What motivated her to offer all she had to live on? Was she afraid to give so much? What would happen to her tomorrow? The story doesn't say what happened to her, but what she did sure pleased God. She lived with confidence that God cares for her, that the One who made her would provide for her needs.

I want to be more like this widow. I want to live with trust in God's ability to care for me, and the understanding that offering myself and my stuff back to God is a simple way to declare, "You are worthy of my trust."

Something to Think About:

1. What do you think was going through the mind of the widow who gave all she had?
2. How do you currently feel about the role money plays in your life and decisions?
3. What ways has God used money or possessions to disciple you during in DTS and since then?

Action Steps:

1. Evaluate the way you spend your money. What does the way you spend your money say about your top five priorities? How about the way you spend your time? Is there anything you'd like to adjust in this regard? Ask God about it.
2. Go without a latte, slurpee and bag of chips, or new nail polish today and give that money to an organization or a missionary you know. Trust me, no gift is insignificant.
3. Read the short story "The Rich Family in Our Church" by Eddie Ogan. It's available on online. Search for it on Google.

Going Deeper:

1. Consider observing a "Buy Nothing" week. For the next week, make a decision you will buy nothing (apart from necessities like groceries, gas, etc.). What do you notice about yourself as a result of this challenge?
2. Watch the classic film *Babette's Feast*, about how an act of extravagant generosity touches the inhabitants of a small village in Denmark.

Day 55 - Keep Looking Ahead

Read: Mark 13:1-13

Reflection:

A few years ago, for the first time in my life, I had the awful experience of getting car sick. I was shocked that something so basic as riding down the road in a bus could have such a powerful effect on my stomach. Where did that come from?

As soon as I was back home, I did some research about what causes motion sickness, and how to prevent it. I learned it's caused when your brain receives conflicting signals. For example, your eyes sense you're staying still, but your inner ear (balance) senses you're in motion. Your brain wants to tell you something is wrong, and nausea is a quick way to get your attention.

To prevent motion sickness, sit in a place where you can see the road ahead of you. When your eyes and your ears can track the movement of the vehicle, your brain is able to make sense of all the input it receives, and you're back in business.

In this passage, Jesus warns the disciples about dangers they will face. Soon the entire world will be groaning and shaking. Wars, famines, earthquakes. People betraying one another. They will be arrested, jailed, questioned, and even put to death. They will experience jolts, bumps, unexpected turns, and it won't feel good. But they mustn't worry or be afraid. Instead they must look ahead—far enough down the road to keep perspective and maintain equilibrium.

I wish Jesus had told them there was a way to avoid the

pain and suffering of the world. I wish He'd given them a solution that made all the bad stuff disappear. Instead, He explains they have a part to play in God's restoration of the world. They are the light. They are the equipment. They will represent God to every people and nation.

When the disciples are freaking out, Jesus reminds them of foundational truths we all need to hear. Don't be afraid. You are not alone. You are part of God's rescue operation on earth. The gospel must be declared to all nations.

When you feel disoriented, upset, and confused by what you see and sense around you, turn your eyes to God. Let Him be your centre and your stability.

Something to Think About:

1. What are some of the things in the world right now that are of concern to you? How do you find yourself responding to what you see and hear?
2. What in this passage is confusing to you?
3. Have you faced trials or persecution because of your faith? How did you sense God with you during that time?

Action Steps:

1. Re-read this passage and make a list of the commands of Jesus. How can these commands apply to your life and situation today?
2. Are there any situations in your life right now where you need to be on your guard? What does that look like? Next time you are about to meet up

with a non-Christian friend or family member, take a few minutes to pray that God would prepare you and give you the words to say—or the humility to listen and learn from them.

Going Deeper:

1. During your DTS outreach, were you able to minister among an unreached people group? If so, take an hour or two to learn more about their history and culture. At the end of your research time, pray for the gospel to be preached and known in that place.
2. One of the best ways for me to gain perspective on life is to get outside and go for a walk. Find some time this week to get into nature, just you and God. The goal is not to walk a long distance or to climb a high mountain. Take this opportunity to look and see what is around you. Pay attention to the trees, rocks, water, sky, animals or flowers you see. Ask God to speak to you through what you see, touch, smell and so on.

Day 56 - Sunday Reflection

We started this week considering the role anger can play in our lives: highlighting the value of something and showing us where there are inconsistencies between what is and what ought to be. We thought about what it means to be an image-bearer of God, representing Him to everyone we meet. We remembered how easy it is to let the fear of what might happen steal the joy and blessings of today. We reflected on the idea of love—how it is both complex and simple—and how it is something worth learning about and growing in. We talked about the connection between trusting God and the way we spend our money. We closed the week reflecting on Jesus' words to the disciples that trials and hardships will come, and when they do, we can look to Holy Spirit for help, remembering we are part of God's plan of restoration.

Sabbath Review: Week Eight

1. Connection. In the past week, who have you connected with? Think about family members, roommates, friends from DTS, people at church, work or school friends. How did you feel about the quality of the time you spent together? How well did you listen? Is there anything that could have made the time together better?

For the coming week, make a point to talk with someone important to you about something you are learning through this devotional book.

2. Service and Generosity. In what ways have you expressed a heart of service and generosity this week? Being willing to serve is a great way to express gratitude and love to others. Service and generosity can look like washing the dishes, taking out the garbage, giving someone a ride somewhere, or asking someone about their day and listening with your full attention. Service and generosity can look like colouring with a child, calling your grandma to say "hello," letting someone ahead of you in the grocery line, or letting someone else decide which movie to watch.

For the coming week, stir up your creativity to bake or cook something and share what you've made with people in your life.

3. Self-care. How have you been taking care of yourself this week? Have you been getting enough sleep? Are you eating well? Are you drinking enough water? What are you doing for exercise? Have you made time for "play," for things you find truly enjoyable: things so fun for you that you lose track of time when doing them? (This could be reading, sports, crafting, hanging out with friends, you name it.)

For the coming week, take a couple hours to participate in a creative activity you enjoy. This could be baking a pie, going dancing, writing a poem, working on your car, building something, taking photos, etc.

4. Spiritual Life. In what ways have you been able to connect with God this week? Where have you sensed His presence as you go about your daily life? Which habits (such as reading Scripture, worship, prayer, Bible study, etc.) have you been able to engage in? What do you sense God is saying to you these days? In what ways do you sense His encouragement and affirmation of you as His child?

For the coming week, ask God to show you how He feels about various people in your life, perhaps those you are closest to or those you are struggling to connect with.

Week Nine

Day 57 - The Line Between Preparation and Compulsion

Read: Mark 13:14-32

Reflection:

I TRAVEL A LOT EACH YEAR, and I've got my routine all sorted out. Packing list, suitcase, carry-on, boarding, fasten seatbelt, unfasten seatbelt, get off plane, pick up luggage, repeat. Along with that, I keep track of passport, travel insurance, house keys, photocopy of passport, photocopy of travel insurance. I also make sure I have my Visa card, MasterCard, bank card, debit card—just in case something happens. Local currency, foreign currency, some US cash, and Euros thrown in for good measure.

Anyone observing my travel preparations would conclude

I'm planning a very long trip or am overly worried something bad will happen to me. Where's the line between wise preparation and fearful compulsion? How much planning is required to make me feel secure enough to step out of my comfort zone?

Sometimes I find myself putting my security and trust in the wrong thing—cards, cash, and planning. I hang my hope and confidence on things and relationships that don't last. The God of the universe says He loves me and promises to take care of me, but I look to my bank balance, resume, or travel insurance for comfort instead.

Jesus knew the disciples would face challenges and trials once He was gone. He was aware of the confusion and chaos around them. Instead of giving specific instructions for what to do in each situation, He reminded them of His Word and the faithfulness of His character.

Whether you are in a situation that is new or unfamiliar, peaceful or chaotic, hopeful or frightening, you can hold on to the promise that God is with you. He is at work around you. Take courage and trust in Him.

Something to Think About:

1. What kinds of things do you look to for security and safety? Is there an amount of money, friends, food, etc. that you never want to be without?
2. What are some experiences you had in DTS or since then that have shown you God is trustworthy?
3. Can you think of a time in your DTS when you

held on to the Word as a source of security and hope? What difference did that make in your life?

Action Steps:

1. Ask Holy Spirit for a revelation of what it means to rely on and depend on God at all times.
2. Find a scripture that was significant to you during DTS (or since then). Write or print it out and post it somewhere you can see it. Heaven and earth will pass away, but God's word lasts forever.

Going Deeper:

1. Read Matthew 6:19-21. What can we learn about security and safety from these verses?
2. Watch a historical movie or war movie and consider that those who had so much power and influence at that time are no longer with us. What does this mean for you?

Day 58 - You Are Still On Active Duty

Read: Mark 13:33-37

Reflection:

I'd been living in a YWAM dorm for a couple years when a friend asked me to car-and-apartment-sit while she went on an outreach. I was thrilled. A car! A kitchen! My own bathroom! So much freedom! So little time!

During the two weeks of house-sitting I reverted to my inner slob, and it felt great. Dishes filled the sink. Clothes were everywhere. My craft projects had space of their own. I never made my bed.

That is, until it was time for her to come back.

I'd wanted to really enjoy my last weekend at my friend's place, but instead I spent a very stressful few days cleaning like a mad woman. I had drastically under-estimated how much effort it would take to clean up after myself. How had I made such a mess?

I wished I'd cleaned a little bit every day and controlled the chaos rather than waited until the last minute. A smidgen of self-control spread over a couple of weeks would have reduced my stress and made housesitting way more fun.

I don't know what you've been up to since DTS ended. I hope you've enjoyed the freedom you've had without falling into the trap of making a huge mess like I did.

For many people, the months after DTS are stressful. The waiting and unknowns can make it hard to enjoy what you have now. Or you might have already made decisions and are working hard at the next thing.

Regardless of what you're waiting for or what you're busy with, it's vital to remember you are still on active duty. You have been sent to represent God to the world. Everything you learned in DTS—prayer, hospitality, loving your enemy, hearing God, serving others—can be put into practice now. The end of DTS doesn't end your growth or your ministry. In fact, life after DTS is very much like being on outreach, but on this outreach, *you* are the leader.

The weekend cleaning frenzy I told you about wasn't motivated by fear. It came from a desire to express love to my friend and make sure her apartment was in perfect shape for her return. It woke me up to the importance of self-control and responsibility.

What if you viewed this post-DTS season from that perspective?

No matter what you're doing—work, school, volunteering, or waiting for direction—you have the chance to live for God in all you do. You don't have to be afraid of a crisis or deadline. Do what you can each day. Stay alert and keep your eyes open. You have so much to give!

Something to Think About:

1. How has your day-to-day life changed since the end of DTS? How do you feel about these changes?
2. In what ways do you think life after DTS is like an outreach where you are the leader?
3. How do you generally deal with seasons of waiting? Do you get anxious, tense, bored, lazy, distracted?

Action Steps:

1. Take some time to review the way you've been spending your time since the end of DTS. Consider your work, friendships, and leisure time. How have you been staying connected to God? How have you been spending your money? How are you stewarding your physical and mental health? Are there any adjustments you'd like to make?
2. Are there any practical things in your life you've been neglecting that could use some attention? How clean is your room? Your kitchen? Your desk? Your yard? Are there any odd jobs, repairs, or tasks you need to do? Consider how you could move forward with some of these, as a step of responsibility and as a sign of your gratitude toward God.

Going Deeper:

1. Read through Acts. It records the lives of those living in the immediate aftermath of Jesus' death who understood the urgency of telling others the good news of what Jesus had done. Two thousand years later, some of that urgency seems to have been lost. As you read Acts, pay attention to the enthusiasm and drive of these early disciples. What can you learn from their attitude and actions?

Day 59 - The Meaning Behind the Gift

Read: Mark 14:1-11

Reflection:

The Bible surprises me with stories of seemingly insignificant people who are examples of faith, extravagance, and love. Jesus commends women and men for their choices, helping us understand what's good and right in His eyes.

We don't have the names of who was at Simon's dinner, but their reaction to the woman with the perfume reveals much about their opinion of Jesus. They viewed her offering as foolish. Why waste something so valuable on a poor rabbi without status or title? Selling the perfume would have given her a bigger bang for her buck, they said.

The dinner guests didn't understand how worthy Jesus was or why anointing Him for burial was significant. But Jesus saw her, her offering, and Himself in a clear light. He honoured her in the presence of those who scolded her and He promised her gift would be remembered.

Gifts are a way to put something intangible like affection, gratitude, or love into physical form. We are to give our lives, our hearts, our strength, and our love to God as an offering. What that looks like and how it is expressed will be unique for each person. Sometimes you and God will be the only ones who understand the value of what you've given.

Like the woman, you may be criticized for what you offer.

There may be people who don't understand what your life is about. They will laugh at you. They will say you're foolish. They will call you a do-gooder or a religious nut.

What we can learn from this woman is how to put our trust in the One who sees and understands the love behind our offering. This woman was convinced of Jesus's worth, and she gave freely and courageously, not fearing for her future or ashamed of her love.

When people question your loyalty and choices, stand secure in what you know about Christ. He sees your offering, and He knows your heart. He won't forget your sacrifices or your love. They are precious to Him.

Something to Think About:

1. If you'd been at the dinner that night, how would you have responded to the woman's offering?
2. How do you feel about gift-giving in general? Do you enjoy it? Hate it? When do you find it difficult or easy to give a gift?
3. Have you ever been criticized or questioned about a gift you've given? What was going on in that situation? What did you learn through the experience?

Action Steps:

1. Be intentional to give a gift to God today. Spend some time thinking about what He might like, what would be meaningful to both of you, what

would bring Him joy. Once you decide on a gift, go ahead and present it to Him.

2. Gift giving isn't just about what we can give or do for God. God Himself is an extravagant giver. Sometimes we take for granted what He's given to us, and forget how great His love is toward us. Take some time to reflect on the gifts God has given to you. Make a list, write a poem, or do something creative that will help you remember God's generous gifts in your life.

Going Deeper:

1. Watch the 1972 film *Brother Sun, Sister Moon.* It is about St. Francis of Assisi and how an encounter with Christ changes the direction of his life, leading to a lifestyle of sacrifice and love. The film is over two hours long, so make sure you have some snacks and a box of Kleenex.
2. Read Ann Voskamp's book, *One Thousand Gifts*, about the author's journey to chronicle the gifts of God in her life.

Day 60 - It Seemed Like A Normal Dinner At The Time

Read: Mark 14:12-31

Reflection:

Can you imagine what it would have been like to eat supper with the disciples that night? You're there chatting and hanging out, no clue that particular meal will become the most talked about meal in history. For the disciples it was a normal Passover, a feast they enjoyed every year at that time.

The disciples arranged the room and food just as Jesus requested. Together with Him they participated in the meal, a retelling of how God rescued Israel out of slavery and brought them into freedom. Jesus poured His heart out to his friends, knowing betrayal and death was coming. As they ate and drank, they didn't realize an even bigger rescue operation was taking place in their midst. It was a special meal for them, a time of connection and intimacy; but it was a *normal* Passover.

When I was twenty-three, I was serving as a staff member with YWAM in the US. A very normal staff meeting one afternoon changed the direction of my life. During announcements, I heard about a team in a restricted access nation that needed English teachers to join their project. Without pause or fuss, I turned to the woman next to me and stated, "I'm going to go there!"

Six weeks later, I was on a plane to a country I was still learning to pronounce. I lived with a local non-believing family and shared Jesus with people who didn't know Him yet. I was trained to teach English, and discovered I loved it. It was an amazing year!

As I look back on the day I went to staff meeting, I see there was nothing special about it. I was going along, doing what I normally did, never imagining how the Spirit would lead me or how significant that announcement would be for my future.

Taking a DTS was a significant event in your life. There were plenty of people and experiences that left a mark on you. Whether you realized it or not, what you experienced at DTS has changed the course of your life. The results of these changes will impact your life and the generations to come!

Each day, no matter how normal, can hold life-changing experiences or encounters which you don't realize at the time. Then, years later, you look back and see how the dots are connected and how God has been directing your life.

Something to Think About:

1. In what ways was God at work in your life to lead you to DTS?
2. Can you think of any events or conversations during DTS that seemed "normal" at the time but turned out to be significant?
3. Think of three memorable conversations during your DTS. Re-live them in your mind and reflect on what you learned through them.

Action Steps:

1. Plan to have a meal with a friend this coming week. Don't worry about it being fancy or expensive. Ask God to make it a meaningful time together.
2. Take some time to think about what you would

want to say to your closest friends or family if you knew you would never see them again. Are there any of those things that you would like to say to them now? What's stopping you from doing so?

Going Deeper:

1. Read the story of Passover in Exodus 12:1-28. Think about the significance of Jesus offering Himself as the sacrifice to keep us from death.
2. Read 1 Corinthians 11:23-26 about the new covenant Jesus created for us.
3. Check out the video "Sacrifice and Atonement" at thebibleproject.com: God's "covering" over human evil through animal sacrifices ultimately point to Jesus and his death and resurrection.

Day 61 - He Chose To Be Vulnerable

Read: Mark 14:32-42

Reflection:

Years ago, just hours after a break-up with a boyfriend, I got a phone call from a friend who had no idea what had happened. She asked about my day, and for a split second I wondered if I could keep my voice steady, pretend everything was okay, and cry the weekend away before revealing my changed relationship status.

Who wants to have their rejection and pain put on display? Who wants to appear weak and needy?

Thankfully, on that day I was able to take a risk towards deeper connection with my friend. I chose to share the news with her. Thirty minutes later she was on my couch, crying with me.

This dramatic example reveals a pattern in my life. When I'm struggling spiritually or emotionally, my tendency is to pull away from people and work through my stuff alone. I'm afraid people will think I'm "unspiritual" if I am struggling. I prefer to look strong and together, and I'm terrified I will be rejected if people see the broken parts of me.

Jesus shows us a different way to live. Jesus was vulnerable enough to ask His close friends to be at His side as He prayed and wept. Jesus was persistent in His request. He didn't drop a hint and hope His friend would figure out what He was asking for. He was specific, persistent, and "needy." Wanting to have people with Him didn't mean His relationship with God was weak. No one has ever had a better relationship with the Father than Him.

If Jesus was willing to ask for help and support from friends when He needed it, what keeps us from being like that too? If Jesus, the perfect human, was able to expose His pain, was willing to lean on others when He felt weak, was willing to admit His fear and grief, then we might have some adjustments to make.

Something to Think About:

1. When you are struggling, are you more likely to share your challenges with people or to withdraw?
2. When's the last time you cried in front of a friend? What was the situation that brought you to tears? How did it feel to be open and vulnerable before them?
3. What thoughts, feelings, or fears keep you from asking for help when you are in need?

Action Steps:

1. Do you have any friends or family members who are going through a challenge right now (loss of relationship, sickness, discouragement, etc.)? Contact them and offer to be a listening ear. When you listen, *only* listen and share their pain. Don't give advice, clichés, or your opinion. Let your presence be a sign of your love and care.
2. Think about your current friendships. Which ones of them would you like to develop into deeper friendships? Next time you are together, take a risk and share something a bit deeper than you have shared before. Ask God to grow and deepen this relationship.

Going Deeper:

1. Check out the book, *Practicing the Presence of People,*

by Mike Mason.

2. Do a word study on "friend." Start with these verses to get you going: Exodus 33:11, 1 Chronicles 20:7, Proverbs 17:17, Proverbs 18:24, Luke 7:34, Luke 11:5-6, James 2:23.
3. Check out Brené Brown's TED talk, "The Power of Vulnerability." It is one of the most watched TED talks of all time.

Day 62 - Where There's Friendship, There's Disappointment

Read: Mark 14:43-52

Reflection:

Can you remember the last time you were betrayed by a friend? I haven't experienced anything like Jesus did, but I've put my trust in someone and been disappointed before. Betrayal and disappointment have a similar sting. You expect one thing and are shocked when reality is different. One minute you feel safe and cared for, and the next minute you're drowning in anger and shock.

Most of us will never be betrayed in a life-and-death situation. We won't have to forgive a friend for turning us over for execution. So then, what can we learn from Jesus' example?

What I see in Jesus is His ability to keep a soft, open heart toward people, even while experiencing betrayal and many painful disappointments. When you open yourself to others, you open yourself to being hurt.

At the end of a summer outreach, my teammates and I were all departing at different times. I was expecting a send-off with prayer, hugs, and lots of affirmation. Instead my closest friend told me she wouldn't be getting up early to say goodbye. I was crushed. I had expected so much more. How could she be so uncaring? Wasn't our friendship important to her?

This experience was a lesson for me about expectation, disappointment, and forgiveness. There are times when friends won't behave the way I want. When that happens, I can choose bitterness, closing my heart to protect it, or I can choose gratitude for what the friend has given and then release her from further expectations.

You may be feeling some relational disappointments right now. When you said goodbye to your DTS friends, you agreed to stay in touch. You might have planned Skype dates and a reunion. But things have changed since then. Some friends don't respond to your messages. Some don't come to gatherings. Some don't make time to ask how you're doing. That can hurt.

Jesus must have felt so disappointed and sad that night. His friend Judas promised one thing but did the opposite. Jesus had poured so much into this friendship, but Judas chose money and personal gain over friendship.

Even at the moment of betrayal, with the sadness and shock of disappointment all around Him, Jesus chose to love and forgive. What amazing strength He displayed! He can help us to do the same when we need it.

Something to Think About:

1. How do you deal with disappointment? Do you respond with anger, resentment, or something else?
2. Do you need to adjust your expectations regarding relationship with any of your DTS friends? If so, what needs to change?
3. Have you ever been the one to betray someone you love? Can you remember the circumstances of that experience and the feelings that went along with it?

Action Steps:

1. Ask God to show you His perspective on the situations from the questions above. How does He feel about these events and the hurt you experienced?
2. Ask God to examine your heart and show you if there is any bitterness, anger, or resentment you still need to deal with. Give these disappointments to the Lord. If you'd like to, ask a friend to pray with you for God to heal you and set you free from the pain you are carrying.
3. Take some time to review the relationships in your life—family, friends, DTS friends, etc. Is there consistency between what you say and how you act? Does anything need to change in your relationships?

Going Deeper:

1. Consider watching *The Passion of the Christ*, if you haven't seen it before.
2. Watch another movie that touches on the topic of betrayal and forgiveness, such as *Les Miserables*.

Day 63 - Sunday Reflection

We started out the week with a reminder that God and His love for us will last forever. The months after DTS can be confusing and stressful, but wherever you are right now is a place God can use you. Not everyone will understand the decisions you are making. Not everyone will understand the love behind your choices. Life is made up of many normal days and lots of ordinary choices. God is with us in the ordinary, and He promises to lead and guide us as we look to Him.

We considered Jesus' willingness to be open and vulnerable with His friends during a time of grief and pressure. We ended the week with the reminder that friendships often involve disappointment and pain. How grateful I am that Jesus is acquainted with joy and disappointment. He can show us how to stay tender towards others, how to forgive those who have hurt us, and He can heal the pain in our hearts.

Sabbath Review: Week Nine

1. Connection. In the past week, who have you connected with? Think about family members, roommates, friends from DTS, people at church, work or school friends. How did you feel about the quality of the time you spent together? How well did you listen? Is there anything that could have made the time together better?

For the coming week, consider being open and vulnerable with a safe friend about something in your life you are struggling with.

2. Service and Generosity. In what ways have you expressed a heart of service and generosity this week? Being willing to serve is a great way to express gratitude and love to others. Service and generosity can look like washing the dishes, taking out the garbage, giving someone a ride somewhere, or asking someone about their day and listening with your full attention. Service and generosity can look like colouring with a child, calling your grandma to say "hello," letting someone ahead of you in the grocery line, or letting someone else decide which movie to watch.

For the coming week, give some "service coupons" to people in your life (for example: This coupon is good for one afternoon of babysitting. This coupon is good for vacuuming the house. This coupon is good for raking the leaves in the yard. This coupon is good for washing your car).

3. Self-care. How have you been taking care of yourself this week? Have you been getting enough sleep? Are you eating well? Are you drinking enough water? What are you doing for exercise? Have you made time for "play," for things you find truly enjoyable: things so fun for you that you lose track of time when doing them? (This could be reading, sports, crafting, hanging out with friends, you name it.)

For the coming week, take time to re-watch a favourite movie or re-read a favourite book.

4. Spiritual Life. In what ways have you been able to connect with God this week? Where have you sensed His presence as you go about your daily life? Which habits (such as reading Scripture, worship, prayer, Bible study, etc.) have you been able to engage in? What do you sense God is saying to you these days? In what ways do you sense His encouragement and affirmation of you as His child?

For the coming week, as you eat meals with family or friends do your best to be present with them around the table. Consider what a gift it is to be with these specific people at this specific time in history. You never know which of the seemingly normal meals or chats may be significant in your life or the life of someone else down the road.

Week Ten

Day 64 - The One Friend Who Stuck Around

Read: Mark 14:53-72

Reflection:

WHEN YOU'RE with your team, prepared, confident, and ready for what's planned, it's possible to stand strong and be bold about your faith. On stage, wearing matching T-shirts, invited to give a presentation about God, it's easy to speak calmly and answer questions with confidence.

However, when the questions are unexpected, backed with malice, or when the person asking them has a face hardened in anger, it's a different story.

How can the strength and confidence I feel when I'm surrounded by others evaporate and be replaced by fear and waffling when I'm alone? What is it about being with others that brings confidence and inspires courage? Why can't I muster up the same nerve when I'm talking with someone at work by myself? With all my training, shouldn't I be better at declaring Christ? What's wrong with me?

I don't blame Peter for his denial of Christ, and I'm not going to point my finger at him. Think about it: he hadn't read the end of the story. He didn't know Jesus would rise from the dead. He didn't know about Easter Sunday or Pentecost. His life hadn't been changed by the indwelling of Holy Spirit. He was a guy who'd eaten a huge meal and gone to a garden with his friends. He'd been taking a nap and was woken up by his mentor right before armed soldiers arrested him. Peter didn't have time to process it all and do a quick Bible study on Messianic prophecies.

It's the middle of the night, and Peter is trying to hold it together. Everyone else has bailed on Jesus, but Peter alone stuck with Him. He was being forced to re-think everything he thought he knew about Jesus, God's Messiah. This was not what Peter had expected to happen.

I've never been in a situation like that. I've never experienced such violence, loss, betrayal, and confusion. If I ever do, I hope I'll be half as brave and loyal as Peter was that night.

Maybe instead of seeing this story as one of denial and failure, we can see it as a story about the courage of a friend who was scared out of his wits and a lesson about how we need each other, especially in times of crisis. Though Peter was powerless to help Jesus in any way, he stuck around as best as he could, watching, hoping, and praying for divine rescue.

Something to Think About:

1. What do you notice about yourself when you are with other Christians compared to when you are by yourself?
2. Can you remember the last time you let down a friend? What happened? What did it feel like?
3. How would you put into words the feeling of being surrounded by friends and teammates during DTS? What does it feel like not to have that now?

Action Steps:

1. What kinds of situations do you find yourself in today when you wish you had a team around you? What could you do to improve these situations?
2. Are there any believers in your work, school, or neighbourhood? How could you find them if they're there? Consider starting a prayer meeting or Bible study with others.

Going Deeper:

1. Doing life together is an amazing part of being a Christ follower! If you'd like deeper fellowship and connection with Christians where you are now, start an online conversation with some DTS friend to brainstorm creative possibilities for gathering people and building community.

Chances are, you're not the only ones looking for opportunity to connect and be encouraged.

2. What are some films, books, or TV shows that have taught you about friendship? Next time you have the opportunity to re-read or re-watch one of these favourites, ask Holy Spirit to deepen your understanding of the love, commitment, and forgiveness that make friendship so precious.

Day 65 - Prayer & Mocking

Read: Mark 15:1-21

Reflection:

One of my favourite outreaches while living in Vancouver was "Prayer Stations." We'd put red vests over our rain coats and head out to stand on a street corner with a cardboard sign saying "Free Prayer." We'd smile a lot and offer to pray for whoever was willing to let us do just that. I loved having a reason and a context to talk with complete strangers about life, prayer, and God. At first I thought no one would be interested in praying together on a street corner, but I was pleased by how many people would stop to pray or chat.

Not all the encounters were warm and friendly, however. Occasionally there were rude comments or cuss words. One day a group of guys stopped to tell us we were naïve and stupid for believing in and following a God who was dead. I was surprised by how angry they sounded and by how differently they viewed the God whom I'd come to love and respect. I felt attacked, mocked, and angry.

Part of why I felt angry was I didn't have the space to explain what I believed or why it was important to me. It never crossed my mind to make space for them to explain what they believed or saw as important. Without knowing anything about them, without sharing my name or asking a single question, I'd decided they were my enemy—and God's enemy. How wrong I was! Seeing someone as an "enemy" makes it very difficult to listen to them with an open heart.

As I reflect on that day, I'm reminded there's much more going on in every person's life than what I can see. Each of us have a story that is complex and nuanced. I don't know what experiences those men may have had with Christians—how they may have been abused or betrayed in God's name. Perhaps their anger was a symptom of an old, deep pain.

If I could go back to that day and do it over again, I hope I could be less offended by what they said and more open to listening and asking questions. Instead of feeling pressure to defend my view, I'd do my best to trust the living Christ at work in every heart, whether I see it or not.

Something to Think About:

1. Have you ever felt mocked, looked down on, or criticized for your belief in Christ? How did you feel when this happened? What were your thoughts about the person who mocked you?

2. How easy is it for you to listen to people who think differently or see the world differently from you? Is there anything you would like to change or adjust about your approach?
3. What do you think it is about the message of God that stirs up such strong emotions in people—in believers who feel like they're defending that message, or in non-believers who express anger or hurt in response to that message?

Action Steps:

1. When you hear or see things you think are anti-God, ask God for His help to let go of defensiveness and argumentativeness, and instead to listen. Ask Him to help you to bless and forgive, just as Christ did on the cross.
2. Are there any people in your life right now who have a habit of being rude to you about your faith? If so, you can do two things. First, you can ask God to help you forgive them and pray a blessing over them. Second, you can take some action to bring more health to the relationship. Share how their rudeness makes you feel. Explain that you think it's important to treat each other's beliefs with respect. It takes courage to lovingly confront someone who is hurting you, but it's important!

Going Deeper:

1. Listen to the voices of people who have been hurt

by Christianity. Can you understand where their anger is coming from? If you have a friend or family member who has been burned by the Church, consider asking if they'd be willing to share their thoughts with you. If they share, just listen. Don't argue or try to fix or correct them. Thank them for sharing. It's scary for a non-believer to tell a passionate believer about doubts or frustrations (or betrayals) they have experienced in the Church.

Day 66 - Bargains & Demands

Read: Mark 15:22-32

Reflection:

It's amazing how God gives us life and breath and everything we need, yet our list of demands never stops:

Prove yourself.

Show your power.

Fulfill your promises.

Do what I ask.

Often it's easier to think about what we don't have instead of being in awe of all we have been given.

Many people are waiting for God to give them a spectacular sign to prove He exists. Healing from an illness, winning the lottery, a promotion at work, restoration of a relationship, peace on earth, or something else.

We bargain and demand, "If you are really there, God, do this for me and I'll believe in you." We want evidence and proof. We want God to perform for us. Sometimes we are so focused on what we want that we are blind to what's right in front of us.

Those standing in front of Jesus were focused on criticism and mockery, entertained by the sight of His suffering and anguish, caught up in the political and religious scandal of His execution. Meanwhile the One who had lived a perfect life was pouring out His blood for their sake, and they couldn't see it. The sacrifice of Jesus on their behalf passed by unacknowledged and unnoticed.

I wonder how often the same thing happens in my life?

Something to Think About:

1. When you first met Jesus, was it through an amazing miracle or something less dramatic?
2. Do you ever find yourself wishing God would do *more* to prove Himself to you?
3. What lessons have you learned during times when God didn't immediately answer your prayers?

Action Steps:

1. What things have you seen God do in your life—during DTS and since then? Try to make a list of fifty things to be grateful for.

2. Spend today only thanking God for who He is and what He's done, not asking for anything. How does it feel?

Going Deeper:

1. Read *Miracles* by C. S. Lewis.
2. Read *The Day the Revolution Began* by Tom Wright.

Day 67 - Truly He is the Son of God

Read: Mark 15:33-47

Reflection:

Two weeks after my DTS ended I flew to Australia to attend another YWAM training course. I was a new believer, with a lot to learn. I tried to soak in everything I could, but I felt the overwhelming sense I would never know enough. I felt so far behind. Many afternoons I would walk home with tears streaming down my cheeks.

During one lecture, the speaker sent us away to spend time with God. I found a space in the children's playroom of the church and sat on the floor with my Bible and notebook open. I hoped God would finally speak to me in the way I longed for. An audible voice? A vision? I'd heard many stories, and I was prepared for an encounter of my own.

I checked my heart, resisted the enemy, invited God to speak, and waited in silence. I waited. And waited. Was I doing something wrong? I started over again from the beginning. Nothing.

The disappointment, frustration, and confusion I'd been carrying around spilled out with a vengeance. I bawled like a baby. What was wrong with me? Why couldn't I hear His voice? I cried for a long time. There was a lot I'd bottled up inside.

After many tears came a clarity I hadn't expected. I realized I'd been putting my hope in my ability to hear God's voice, not in God Himself. I blew my nose and wiped my eyes. I spoke to God, the devil, and myself: "God, I choose to trust you—not because of what you do for me now or what you might do for me down the road, but because of who you are and what you've already done. Even if I never hear from you, I will continue to follow and love you."

Sometimes it's in the moments of disappointment, seeming failure, or silence that we finally understand something about who Jesus really is. That was the case for me, and for the centurion who watched Jesus on the cross.

I can see God *did* speak to me that day in the toy room. I'm grateful for the anguish of not getting what I wanted, because it revealed the greed and selfishness of my heart.

The cross of Christ teaches us so many things. It reminds us that what we can see and what God is doing may be very different from each other. When I'm tempted to accuse God of not doing what I want, I am learning to lean instead on what I know of His character and ways, and to put my trust in Him still.

Hope in the Lord. Wait on Him. Truly He is the Son of God.

Something to Think About:

1. Can you relate to the story of trying to hear God's voice in the kids' room at the church? What part of the story can you relate to?
2. Have you had times when you thought God was ignoring you, but looking back you see how He was at work in your life at that very moment?
3. Why do you think it is we often have clarity and new insight in times of trial, loss, and pain?

Action Steps:

1. Take a walk with God, leaving your phone and other distractions behind. Reflect on times you've experienced loss, pain, or trials and how you experienced God with you. Just because you didn't hear a voice or see a vision doesn't mean God wasn't there. Ask Him to remind you of His faithful presence with you.
2. Look online for paintings and images of the crucifixion and Jesus on the cross. Let the Holy Spirit speak to you as you are reminded of what Jesus did for us. Pick one of your favorites and save it.

Going Deeper:

1. Francine Rivers has written a great trilogy about life in the Roman Empire right after the death of Christ. Check out *A Voice in the Wind*, *An Echo in the Darkness*, and *As Sure As the Dawn.*

Day 68 - Days, Weeks, Months, Years, Decades, & Centuries

Read: Mark 16:1-20

Reflection:

What an incredible chapter this is! After the confusion and loss of the crucifixion, God triumphs over death by raising Jesus to life. A stone is rolled away; angels speak to humans; the resurrected Jesus appears to His followers while they are walking down the road, and to others at dinnertime. The Great Commission is given, and Jesus ascends. The disciples are filled with courage and power once again, and away they go, revealing God's power through signs and wonders.

A lot can change in a few months!

It's been a few months since your DTS finished, and it's easy to get discouraged if you haven't seen changes or breakthroughs. It's easy to conclude something is wrong. What are you missing?

This is when it's important to look at the larger story of God in His world. Remember the three years Jesus walked with His disciples? Remember the decades Jesus spent working as a carpenter in Nazareth? Remember Israel's decades in the wilderness and centuries of slavery?

The story of God began thousands of years before Christmas and carries on long after Easter. What may feel like a season of pointless waiting is probably not pointless at all. Whatever time and place you are right now is somewhere God is at work. From believer to believer, year after year, through hardships and joy, God continues to partner with His people to spread His message. We are those people.

We are the people Jesus told to go everywhere and tell everyone what He had done. The early disciples had no theology degrees, big budgets, or international connections. They spoke about what they had seen and heard. They talked about how Jesus had changed them.

That's what we are to do now.

When you get tired, discouraged, worn out, or afraid, look to Christ on the cross. Remember the love that motivated His surrender. When your life feels busy, crazy, out of control, or very different from what you expected, take another look at Christ. Look to the empty grave, the stone rolled away by the hand of God.

When you aren't sure what is next for you, or when you can't see where God is in your life, take a closer look at the table where you are eating, the road where you are walking.

Just as Christ surprised His disciples by showing up when

they didn't expect it, He promised to be with us always. And that promise applies to your life, this very day.

Something to Think About:

1. What were the "stones" you faced as you prepared for DTS? How did God roll them away for you?
2. What things in your life right now feel like huge stones to be rolled away?
3. How can you gain perspective by thinking about the three years of training the disciples had, the decades Jesus spent at home, and the history of Israel? What difference does it make to see yourself as part of God's big story?

Action Steps:

1. Make a list of any overwhelming circumstances you are facing right now. How is God showing Himself faithful in the midst of these challenges?
2. Make a timeline of the last two (or five) years of your life, noting of the various "stones" that have blocked your way, or that you feared would block your way. Consider how God has rolled away the stones for you, helping you overcome challenges that were too big for you. Take time to thank God for His faithfulness and ask Him for eyes of faith to see what is ahead of you.

Going Deeper:

1. Watch the 2016 film *Risen* about a Roman soldier's search to locate the missing body of Jesus after His crucifixion.
2. Another great film about the transformative power of the resurrection is the 1959 film, *Ben-Hur*. One of my favourites!

Day 69 - Guard What's Been Given To You

Read: 1 Timothy 6:11-21

Reflection:

For the last devotion of *The Next 70 Days*, I've chosen a passage from 1 Timothy. What an amazing exhortation Paul gives to his young friend! So much great advice. It might sound a lot like the speech your DTS leader gave at your graduation.

When I left DTS, I left behind the best thing I'd ever been a part of. So much had happened. I'd changed drastically. I was incredibly grateful for the friends I'd made. What a gift it was to encounter the living God in the midst of such a vibrant community! I felt I had been ruined for the ordinary.

Since then I've said *hello* and *goodbye* to many, many people. What keeps me from getting crushed by all the goodbyes is knowing God will continue to bring me friends, and that every amazing relationship has to begin somewhere.

I'm not sure what the next seventy days have in store for you, or the seventy days after that. I predict you will have some joy and frustration, some hellos and goodbyes, some days when you feel it's all coming together, and other days when everything seems to be falling apart.

Be of good cheer. Fix your hope on God. He's committed to you for eternity. He will be there for you in every transition, entry, and re-entry.

No matter where you go from here or what the next years of your life hold, you won't go wrong if you put your hope in God! Keep your eyes on eternity. Guard what's been given to you. New adventures await. Let the next chapter begin!

Something to Think About:

1. What does it mean for you to "put your hope in God"?
2. What do you remember about the first day of your DTS? What do you remember about the last day of DTS? What it was like to say goodbye to your DTS friends?
3. Are you happy with who and how you have kept in touch with since DTS ended? Is there anything you'd like to do differently in this regard?

Action Steps:

1. Make a list of ten (or more) things that God has given to you or done for you since you finished your DTS.
2. Consider what you will do for the next ten weeks to stay connected to God and others. Write some action points and goals for yourself (e.g. read one chapter of the Bible each day, Skype with a friend each Sunday, read one Christian book each month, etc.). Put a reminder in your calendar five weeks from now to review how your plan is going.
3. Ask God if there is one person in your circle of relationships that you could encourage to attend a DTS in the future. Give them a call or take them for coffee and seriously present it to them. Be as direct and specific as you are able.

Going Deeper:

1. Paul tells Timothy to pursue righteousness, godliness, faith, love, perseverance, and gentleness. Pick one of these attributes and throw yourself into it for the whole day. See if you can find five ways to exercise it in your thoughts, words, and interactions with others.
2. Get out of bed tomorrow and think about clothing yourself with internal qualities, like kindness, goodness, patience, faith… Imagine for a few minutes what it would look like to put those things on. What would the world see if you did that?

Day 70 - Sunday Reflection

We started this week thinking about how Peter stuck around at Jesus' trial when everyone else ran away. We need people in our lives: not just to fix our problems, but to share our fears and pain. We talked about the temptation to make judgments about others and to defend our views without taking time to listen to or understand each other. We looked at the demands we make of God, wanting more proof and bigger signs instead of noticing what He has already done and who He is.

After the resurrection, the disciples had a hard time grasping what had happened to Jesus. They had a hard time recognizing Him in their midst. This still happens to us today. Just like the disciples walking to Emmaus, we continually need to have our eyes opened to see Jesus alive and in our midst.

As we finish *The Next 70 Days*, let's keep our hearts open to God, expecting and trusting Him to be with us always.

Sabbath Review: Week Ten

1. Connection. In the past week, who have you connected with? Think about family members, roommates, friends from DTS, people at church, work or school friends. How did you feel about the quality of the time you spent together? How well did you listen? Is there anything that could have made the time together better?

For the coming week, set up a time to talk with someone from

DTS. Be sure to ask them how they are doing in this season of life and how you can pray for them.

2. Service and Generosity. In what ways have you expressed a heart of service and generosity this week? Being willing to serve is a great way to express gratitude and love to others. Service and generosity can look like washing the dishes, taking out the garbage, giving someone a ride somewhere, or asking someone about their day and listening with your full attention. Service and generosity can look like colouring with a child, calling your grandma to say "hello," letting someone ahead of you in the grocery line, or letting someone else decide which movie to watch.

For the coming week, practice being aware of and noticing the people around you, whether you are on the bus, in a coffee shop, or at the grocery store. You don't have to talk these people or interact with them; simply pay attention to the people around you. They are precious.

3. Self-care. How have you been taking care of yourself this week? Have you been getting enough sleep? Are you eating well? Are you drinking enough water? What are you doing for exercise? Have you made time for "play," for things you find truly enjoyable: things so fun for you that you lose track of time when doing them? (This could be reading, sports, crafting, hanging out with friends, you name it.)

For the coming week, do something to treat yourself in celebration of completing *The Next 70 Days*. Invite someone to join you in the celebration, if that sounds good to you.

4. Spiritual Life. In what ways have you been able to connect with God this week? Where have you sensed His presence as you go about your daily life? Which habits (such as reading Scripture, worship, prayer, Bible study, etc.) have you been able to engage in? What do you sense God is saying to you these days? In what ways do you sense His encouragement and affirmation of you as His child?

For the coming week, find the painting *The Road to Emmaus* by Janet Brooks-Gerloff online. Meditate on the painting, imagining you had been one of the disciples walking to Emmaus with Jesus, not realizing it was Him.

Epilogue

The DTS After DTS

YOUR DTS LEADER may have told you "DTS never ends," and I agree. The entire life of the Christian is a journey of growth, refining, and transformation. Learning to live like Christ is what our life is about. So whether you've been following Jesus for months or years, we all have the privilege of walking with Him together. Being in a lifelong DTS means *you* get to choose which of the habits, activities, and practices from DTS you will hold on to.

Being able to participate in a DTS was an incredible gift. The friendships, adventures, and growth of DTS were even better than what many of us dreamt. As time goes by, it's easy to put DTS and the people who were part of it on a pedestal. We can cast DTS in such a positive light that no other Christian community, church, or group of friends can compare.

Let me remind you: the people in your DTS were not much different from any other group of Christians with a desire to serve God. They had strengths and weaknesses, off days, annoying habits. What made your DTS friends so special, so amazing in your eyes, is the fact that they were *yours*. They were the group of people with whom you journeyed. They saw you at your worst and at your best. They shared your deep pains and great joys. They laughed and cried with you. Together you grew in God, and the intensity of DTS bonded you together. What a gift it is to have depth of friendship like that! Cherish these relationships and memories as precious gifts from God.

And so now, with DTS behind you, you may be afraid you will never have such close friends again. You may worry about returning to destructive habits or patterns. You might wonder how to stay close to God and how to connect with something as significant as the mission of DTS.

I have felt these things myself, and they are worth thinking about. Asking these questions and wanting to stay connected shows the value you place on God, people, and purpose. Let's use the next 70 days to talk more about these questions. Let's trust God to bring others into our lives who can help us grow. Let's ask Him to open our eyes to see the opportunities to connect and build relationship around us. Let's ask for His help in taking all we've learned in DTS and walking in it—right where we are today. The DTS after DTS is in session!

Acknowledgments

I have to give a big *thank you* to my YWAM Nexia teammates (circa 2011) who were part of the creation of *The 100 Days Project*, which was itself a precursor to *The Next 70 Days*. Wendy McAlpine in particular played a key part in the creation of that project. At that time, twenty different YWAM staff contributed devotionals for a DTS re-entry project that lasted a hundred days. While I have written new content to take the place of what they wrote, I was inspired and encouraged by their insight, creativity, and perspective.

Kim Atkinson, Bobbie Hamm, Cindy Hunt, and Donna MacGowan have helped me hone the question and application section for each day. I'm grateful for your encouragement, suggestions, and input. I've learned so much by watching the way you think and educate.

I'd like to thank my editor, Kay ben-Avraham. Without your help, this book would not be what it is.

Thank you, Liz Waller, for providing moral support

whenever book decisions were making me go crazy. Your perspective and encouragement were a great help.

To all the DTS graduates who gave feedback about these devotionals or who have shared stories from re-entry, I'm grateful for your honesty and trust.

Tanya Lyons